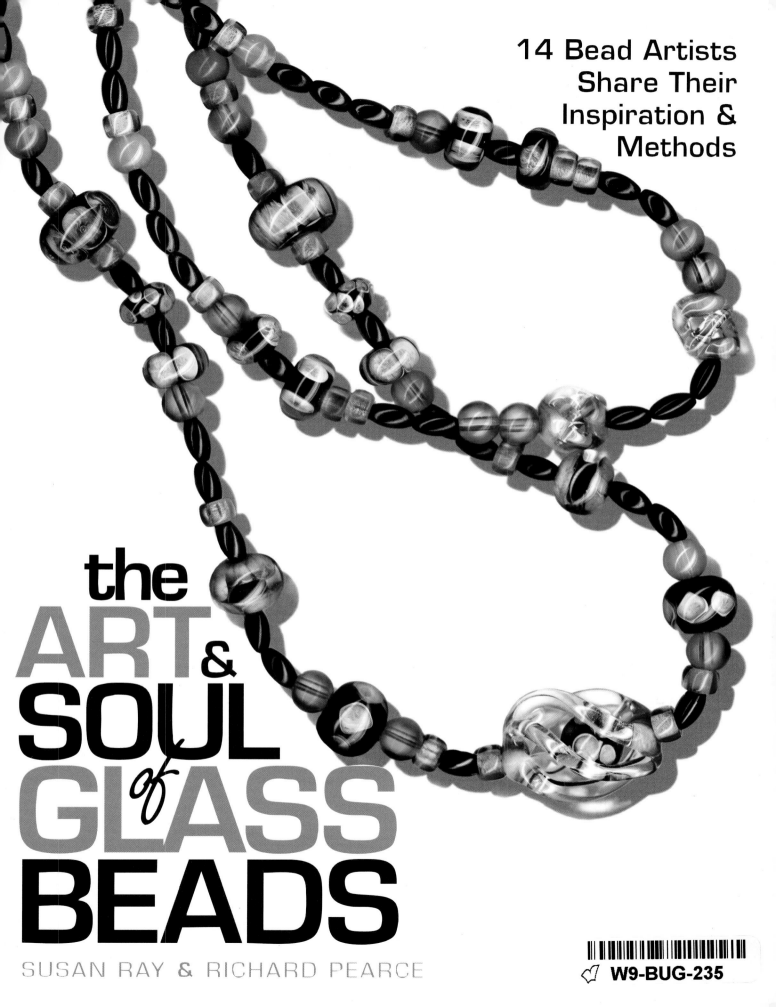

14 Bead Artists
Share Their
Inspiration &
Methods

the ART& SOUL of GLASS BEADS

SUSAN RAY & RICHARD PEARCE

kp **krause publications**
An F&W Publications Company

700 East State Street • Iola, WI 54990-0001
715-445-2214 • 888-457-2873
www.krause.com

Please call or write for our free catalog of publications. To place an order or
obtain a free catalog, please call 800-258-0929 or use our regular business
telephone, 715-445-2214.

Library of Congress Catalog Number 2002113159
ISBN 0-87349-565-9

All photographs by Richard Pearce

**"Entrapment," by Lynn Nurge, appears on the cover and title page of this
book.**

DEDICATION

My parents, both creative in nature, were skilled artisans. My father was a teacher and a master carpenter. My mother was a gifted needle worker. The skill levels they achieved were not nearly as important to them as the task at hand, and their love of doing it. To every project my Dad built, from a child's ant farm to an elegant library bookcase, he brought something of himself. Within each quilt my Mother cross-stitched, she extinguished life's daily tedium, and filled our home with beautiful treasures. But when I look at their handiwork today, I see them in total. I hear my father's laughter. I see my mother's hands as they cross-stitched well into the evening light.

Behind every torch's flame, there is also a story: A human drama. And, too, with each bead, a small piece of that story unfolds. We have been blessed to be able to bring you many fascinating stories, and the artistic photographs of Richard Pearce. I hope you will come to know the artists behind their work. For within each bead lies a piece of their soul.

To my mother and father, who always found time to teach me a new craft.
To my son, Eric, for letting me play Mom even when a store-bought costume would have done just fine.
To Julie and Christine, who nursed us through the long wait to put pen to paper.
To Paula, Noreen, and Sue for their love and caring.
To Pat, Mary Beth, Trent, Barb, Claire, Tamara, Meghan, and Brittany for their words of encouragement and their kind generosity in sharing their own special skills.
To Richard: For the good fortune to have met him, for his skilled eye behind the camera lens, and his kind heart.
Richard, thank you for your unwavering patience and time to take up the challenge to help me bring my personal feelings to the written page.

To Kevin, for letting me have another day.

Susan Ray

CIRQUE DU SOLIEL

Focal beads by Karen Leonardo
Design by Susan Ray

This project was the brainchild of Susan Ray, my co-author and friend. It is to her, then, that the bulk of my gratitude gladly goes. The rest I reserve for my parents and for my fast friends in Santa Barbara and Galena.

Richard Pearce

FOREWORD

In the pages of this book, you will read the stories of some of today's finest lampwork artists. Many of the stories are happy ones, some are sad, but all are full of real, human frailties—and triumphs. These artists readily admit to their mistakes as often as they do to their successes, and they share their struggles: With the glass; with honing a skill once so secretly guarded; with the frustration to find good suppliers, and even to eke out a living by using Internet auctions to reach new patrons. They share, too, their inspiration, their courage, and their strength to pursue their art. One tells a harrowing story of a tragic fire during her childhood, and how glass working helped her overcome her fear of fire and find the courage to light the torch. A few have watched their passion take new roots in a sibling, a spouse, or a child. Others will tell you how their families cope with their obsessions. Throughout these pages, you will get a glimpse into their creative bliss, and share their joy when the flame is lit. Every story is rich with the same "soul" that imbues each bead. Just like the beads that they create, each artist is an individual, and each beautiful.

Although many of our artists are self-taught, each has skillfully mastered this ancient craft. Many admit, rather apologetically, to having found "their own way" of doing things (and they invite us to learn from their trials). They share their relentless pursuit to get "that perfect bead." They share their tips and techniques, suppliers, resources, places to visit, and places to learn. Some will tell you about the cooperative efforts they shared with jewelry designers. Even though all of these artists make beautiful glass beads, few actually make them into jewelry – most focus on forming a bead set from a glass rod or two rather than actually creating the method of adornment.

We hope you will gain insight into the fascination of making glass beads and the jewelry we have created from these tiny masterpieces, as well as an understanding of how this craft is woven into these artists' every-day (and sometimes odd-hours-of-the-night) lives. They share how they secretly plan their next bead at their office, between bottle feedings, or after the "late show." Just as most of us do, they find time for what they love most: Making the next bead.

Our primary goal in creating this book was to capture your interest. In that spirit, we invite you to set sail with us on our voyage to find the "perfect" glass bead. Join us as we reach into the artists' souls and reveal the wonder each of their beads hold; for from the beads in hand forged from their lamps, you will see something of yourself, perhaps, reflected in them. And, we will entice you with a showcase of jewelry projects. Whether you make beads yourself, or purchase them, we hope you will also find yourself paying homage to this art, just as we have, with necklaces, lariats, earrings, and bracelets—many of which are so simple to make, you can complete them in just one evening.

Our secondary goal was to inspire and enlighten you. We hope this book does just that; we have taken the noble challenge to heart. But what we began with—a love affair with a simple rod of glass—evolved into something well beyond that in the hands of these artful human beings: We discovered that we were also celebrating human nature, and we have been irrevocably changed through the experience.

You are about to experience, first-hand, these creative souls' will to give. But, you will be asked to participate—and whether you choose to stand as an observer to the technical skills each artist has obtained, to light the torch yourself, or to string your own set of beads, you will be changed, too, when you complete your journey through these pages.

CONTENTS

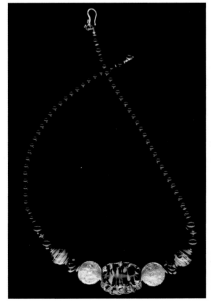

*"Chicory"
photo by
Richard
Pearce*

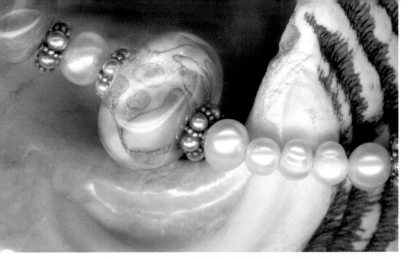

THE QUEST FOR THE 'PERFECT' BEAD

by Tamara Knight

An expert bead maker tells how beads are crafted— and how you can spot superior craftsmanship.

I began making beads in Alaska where bead stores are few and far between. For the most part, I let the flame and heat control what's going on. Usually, I have a design in mind, but I rarely end up with what I imagined because I let myself experiment as I go. If I like a bead, I will then make more to form a set.

In theory, the basic techniques for making glass beads are simple. A mandrel, or iron rod, is covered with a clay-like substance known as a slip or release. This substance helps keep the newly formed glass bead from sticking to the mandrel. A glass rod is then heated under a torch. The end of the glass rod becomes molten and the glass is wound onto the mandrel ever so carefully (another name for lampwork is "wound work"). As the glass passes to the mandrel, the bead maker turns the rod many times until its surface becomes smooth and round.

There are many ways to decorate a bead. Sometimes the bead maker will use additional glass to form lines, shapes, and raised areas.

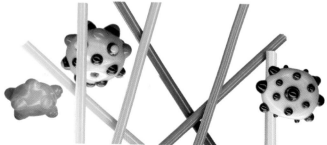

Lampwork glass comes in dozens of strengths and a riot of colors. Expert bead makers know the subtle differences between them. Pictured above is soft Satake glass from Japan.

Other materials can be applied, such as gold, silver, enamel, and Murini. Murini are slices or discs of patterned glass. One type of commonly used Murini is millefiori, which, when translated, means "a thousand flowers."

Beads can also be "cold worked" or decorated after they are away from the torch. Some of these post-torch decorations include etching, sandblasting, electroplating, and faceting.

Glass comes in a variety of strengths, densities, and colors. Shaping the glass into a bead can be done by controlling the melting of the glass against gravity, or using tools such as graphite paddles or marble molds. A marble mold will impart a nice, round quality to a bead and helps control size for matching beads.

All of my beads are kiln annealed, which is a very important step in making a bead that will stand up to the wear and tear of daily use. To anneal a bead, the temperature is raised for several hours, to just below the point at which

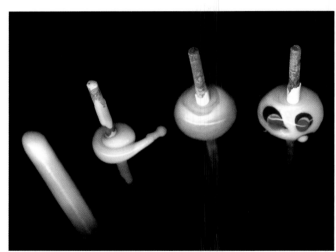

Hot glass is wound around a rod, or mandrel, to begin the bead making process.

glass melts. Over several more hours, the bead is cooled evenly. This process relieves stress in the glass caused by uneven cooling during the production of the bead. Stress is one of the main reasons beads crack. Professional annealing is always done with a kiln.

After the bead has been annealed, the release is cleaned from the holes and any sharp areas are removed. Beads are then separated into sets or singles ready for your project. Many experienced glass artists will mix beads of different glasses to form a single set.

Bead makers who care about their product will be certain to clean the bead hole completely. As you become a bead connoisseur, you will doubtless find other elements that make up the perfect bead. Some of these elements, however, are only a matter of preference. Some bead makers believe, for example, that a good bead should have a puckered hole, and some do not.

Puckered Holes

What is a puckered hole? A puckered hole is an indent around the hole—a feature that is a matter of preference for the buyer. Not so long ago, I felt a puckered hole was the ultimate indication of a perfect bead. The more I talk to bead buyers, though, the less it concerns me. I would say over half of my clients ask for perfectly round beads. The rounder the bead is, the less likely you will see a pronounced pucker. Should you buy beads with puckered holes? Sure … if you like them that way!

Hole Size

The actual size of the bead hole is a consideration when making any jewelry project. Sometimes the hole is too small for some of the stringing materials available, and a hole that is too large may allow the bead to wobble about on the stringing material. One way to remedy a too-large hole is to fill the hole with another bead.

Encasing

An encased bead has a layer of clear glass over the underlying color. The clear glass on encased beads magnifies their inner materials and often distorts the pattern or creates an illusion of inner depth. You may find yourself wondering if the clear layer should go all the way to the hole, or if the small bubbles that can form are to be avoided. While the answers may be a matter of personal preference, I believe that the perfectly encased bead leaves none of the underlying color exposed at the hole, is free from bubbles, and is of even thickness around the core material.

A small unevenness in the encasement, however, or color around the holes may actually add an interesting effect to the design. One of my favorite borosilicate beads has a clear stripe one-third the width down the center; the non-encased ends make up the other two thirds and are clearly visible on each side. When strung with several other similar beads it creates an interesting effect integrating both magnification and an outside oxidation.

Bubbles?

Bubbles can occur spontaneously during the production of the bead, or can be purposely placed for interest. Some types of borosilicate rods are even prized for their micro-bubble "champagne" effect. There is also a technique I enjoy—using baking soda, which causes the glass to encase thousands of random bubbles of various sizes.

Bubbles should be considered part of the design element unless they are so close to the surface as to cause a weak point, or are a distraction to the design or effect of the bead.

Bumpy Beads

Beads with raised bumps are referred to by many different names depending on the pattern of the raised areas, or design they create. When purchasing these beads, look for raised areas that are attached by a larger area that touches the bead than that which actually stands up. Bumps with smaller attached areas or underscores are more likely to be chipped off than bumps with larger attached areas.

Cracks—Always Bad!

Cracks are caused by stress. If glasses are not compatible, they expand and shrink at different rates, causing stress where the two types meet. Beads not properly annealed also contain stress caused by uneven cooling. Do not buy a bead that is already cracked; it will finish cracking sooner or later. Most reputable lampworkers will replace a broken bead that has not been abused.

A good bead must possess at least three technical qualities. First, it must be properly annealed to prevent breakage. Second, it should have no sharp edges that can wear the stringing materials down and cause breakage. Third, the release in the hole must be removed; otherwise, it can act like sandpaper, and may also leave a ring around the neck of the bead or bead wearer.

Should a Good Bead Cost More?

A high price tag does not always mean you're getting the best bead. Don't pass up a bead just because it was made by a beginner. As a beginning bead maker, the artist may have "pushed the envelope" on technique, design, and have a fresh approach to mixing colors. Some of the most interesting beads may not exhibit perfect technical expertise, but the bead may be very artistic and just perfect for your needs! 🌑

You can find Tamara discussing lampworking on the ISGB forum http://www.ISGB.org.

LEARNING TO MAKE THE 'PERFECT' BEAD

The techniques for lampworking have been closely-guarded secrets for centuries. In recent years, several books have been published to revive this ancient art form. *You Can Make Glass Beads* and *Making Glass Beads by* Cindy Jenkins are two highly recommended books. Kate Fowle Meleney has produced several videos for beginning to advanced glass bead artists. This delicate art form is now openly explored, providing new and exciting artistry.

Many glassmakers share their craft with family and friends. Some of the artists who appear in this book offer private classes in their own studios. Some colleges today also offer lampworking classes. Tamara Knight's young boys make beads with their talented mom, and Karen Leonardo's husband has joined her at the torch. Trent Warden encouraged his twin brother, Shawn, to join in, making them an outstanding glass bead making duo. Lampworking is infectious, and the glass beads are a treasured reward. We have seen a real revival of one of the most exciting, highly sought after, wearable art forms.

To become a lampworker, you begin by investing in a basic starter kit. These kits range in price from less than $100 to approximately $500, depending upon the type of torch you choose to purchase. Torches are available in single-fuel models as well as premix and surface-mix designs. A simple multi-purpose torch can produce a heat of 1700 degrees to 1900 degrees. Starter kits include either a Hot Head or Minor burner.

Professional torches require oxygen and propane regulators. Kits also include protective eyewear to prevent flying glass injuries and protect the lampworker from the extremely bright light of the flame. Many kits also include mandrels, a rod rest, tweezers, pliers, and a mandrel release or separator. Glass artists will often add graphite paddles and rakes for shaping and adding designs to their beads. Marvers and other shaping tools are also available. A ceramic fiber-insulating blanket is essential. The blanket prevents thermal stress, and prevents the glass bead from cooling too quickly and cracking.

Once you have begun, you will want to add a kiln. Kilns are expensive but provide a better method of cooling the hot beads and the only way to professionally anneal your beads. Completed beads must be cooled, annealed, and properly cleaned before stringing.

As with all arts and crafts, it is important to understand the proper use of your equipment. Post fire and safety guidelines for use in your home or studio. Set up an area in a dry, well-ventilated environment. Anchor your torch properly. Make sure that your tools are available to you without crossing your torch flame. Set up your kiln in a safe location in your studio. Follow manufacturers' suggested guidelines. Ask for the Material Safety Data Sheet for any products you wish to use. This sheet provides information about the safe use of the material as well as health hazard information. Allow a time to work free of distractions. Always have a fire extinguisher available. Do not ever leave your torch unattended.

The basic techniques for making a glass bead can also be found online through some of the glass suppliers and distributors and glass bead maker organizations such as the International Society of Glass Beadmakers at www.isgb.org. Several top glass suppliers make starter kits available: Arrow Springs Manufacturers, www.arrowsprings.com; Steinert Industries, www.steinertindustries.com; Wheaton Science Products at www.wheatonsci.com and Frantz Art

Glass and Supply at www.frantzbead.com.

The Internet serves as host to buying, selling, trading, and teaching about the art of lampwork. Internet chat groups and boards can provide one-on-one assistance along the way. There are two well-known auction sites at which to sell and buy beads: www.ebay.com (search for "lampwork" or "glass beads") and www.justbeads.com (an auction house devoted to auctions of all types of beads).

Lampwork artists love sharing their knowledge. If you are interested in learning about glass bead making, start by visiting the International Society of Glass Beadmakers at http://www.isgb.org, the Corning Museum at www.cmog.org, and The Bead Museum in Prescott, Arizona at www.thebeadmuseum.com. These Web sites provide an extraordinary wealth of knowledge. Many sites list local guilds and regional organizations as well as lampwork bead shows throughout the country.

Know your glass. Glass for lampworking is available in rods that are usually 6mm in diameter. Glass comes in a variety of opacities, colors, and patterns. Two of the most important elements of glass making are the compatibility of the type of glass rods used and their viscosity. Glass is sometimes compared through a rating system known as the COE. This system explains the coefficient or rate of expansion of the glass. Wheaton Science Products provides more about this rating system and additional glass technology terms at www.wheatonsci.com. The viscosity of the glass is as important as its expansion. A lampwork artist must consider both characteristics. Sometimes it is best to test the outcome yourself. Individual methods of construction and annealing can contribute to the success of the bead maker.

Glass differs when heated, softened, and melted. Glass must be heated slowly to the right temperature. Many glass rods will change color when heated. Some glass rods change color permanently when heated to the proper temperature. Some suppliers sell samplers of glass rods so that you can experiment with the many types of glass available today. The common types of glass include: Moretti, Murano, Satake, Lauscha, Borosilicate, and Bullseye.

Learn about the differences of the glass you plan to use. Remember to combine compatible glass by comparing their COE rating and their viscosity. Ask other lampworkers about their experience with a particular mix of glasses.

Once you have honed the basic skills of lampworking, you will find there is no limit to the possibilities. As you will see with the many fine artists in this book, the love of glass has provided many sources of inspiration for jewelry designers and wearers.

Types of Glass

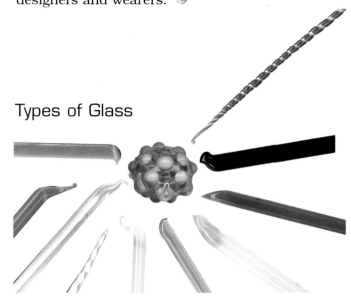

The various types of glass lampworkers use to make ornamental beads are classified based on their relative hardness, a property that in turn is directly related to melting temperature. Thus, a soft glass like Satake melts at a lower temperature and is not as hard or dense as a borosilicate glass (of which Pyrex™ is the best known example). Each type of glass has unique characteristics such that all of them are of interest to the bead maker.

Satake: A soft glass from Japan that is hand-pulled, and is known for its wide array of often unique colors.

Moretti or Effetre: This medium-soft Italian glass is popular among bead makers because of its wide range of colors and relative ease of manipulation under flame.

Lauscha: A medium-soft German glass made especially for flame working.

Bullseye: Slightly harder than Moretti, this glass, which is made by the Bullseye Glass Company of Portland Oregon, is available in an array of opalescent and transparent colors.

Borosilicate: This hard, dense glass passes from the fluid to the hard phase rather quickly, but only at higher temperatures. Bead makers love it for its clarity, durability, and unusual effects.

Dichroic: Literally meaning "two-colored," this glass is impregnated with metal oxides that give it an iridescent quality.

CRANBERRY
CHIFFON

Necklace
Lampwork by Karen Leonardo
Design by Susan Ray

I make my beads in sets. It feels more finished to me than one bead and it tells a story.

—Karen Leonardo, written with Matthew Clasby

Karen Leonardo's passion for lampwork beads started when she was just seven years old—an age at which she was not only allowed but encouraged to dig through her grandmother's jewelry troves. "My grandmother would let me take apart her jewelry pieces and make my own primitive little designs on a string," explains Karen of her early introduction to the field of glass. "That's when I fell in love with jewelry and beads."

Her grandmother, an immigrant from Hungary, was Karen's entrance into the world of creativity. Her grandmother would encourage Karen to explore both her talent and her curiosity. "I would love staying over at my grandmother's house, digging through her jewelry. She was very generous, often donating her most prized pieces for my own creations," Karen recalls.

Karen's father was another big influence in her creative life. He was an inventor with two U.S. patents to his name. "He was very creative and always encouraged me in my younger years to pursue my artistic desires," says Karen. But the pursuit of Karen's promising dreams of glass was to be abruptly interrupted when trauma struck her family.

"As a child, things seemed perfect until my mother was diagnosed with cancer," explains Karen. "My mother died when I was nine, and my father lost everything: His success, his incredible business, and his love for life. After her death, my life revolved around simple survival. I grew up very quickly. At the age of eleven, when I was shopping for groceries for the family, I remember the clerks asked where my parents were. They eventually grew to know who I was. There was a lot of sadness in my young life, but I was soon a master at being strong and suppressing my emotions."

Drawing and beading with her grandmother proved to be a therapeutic outlet for Karen during those years. "When I was a teenager, my thoughts turned to the direction of my life and to college. I wanted to take an artistic route, but I had no role model at the time to guide me in that direction." Instead, Karen took her grandmother's advice and sought a degree in dietetics and nutrition. Karen later married and had three children, but the muse inside kept on calling. In 1993, Karen began making plastic jewelry.

"I was bored and thought I would start a hobby. Having three babies at the time left me yearning for something for myself." Plastics brought Karen back to making jewelry—a medium that she found quick and easy and eventually took her to the world of craft fairs and "art as business."

"My plastic jewelry business became successful, but at craft shows I often heard the comment, 'I could do that myself,' and I became a little resentful."

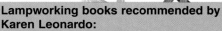

Karen Leonardo

ARTIST'S CONTACT INFORMATION

Karen Leonardo
Just Leonardo
362 Hood School Rd.
Indiana, PA 15701
(724) 357-8709
E-mail: justleo7@ptdprolog.net
Web site: *www.justleonardo.com*
eBay user ID: justleonardo

Lampworking books recommended by Karen Leonardo:
Making Glass Beads
by Cindy Jenkins
The History of Beads
by Lois Sherr Dublin
Contemporary Lampworking
by Bandhu Scott Duham

Good Beads, Bad Beads: Karen's Tips for Finding the Perfect Bead
Good beads are symmetrical with nice ends where the glass meets the mandrel. Raised dots are even. The encasing is clear of bubbles and overall the bead is evenly encased. Bad beads have jagged edges where the bead meets the mandrel or too many bubbles, blackish propane streaks, lop-sided, small fractures, or cracks.

Tip for Coating with Pixie Dust
Put the pixie dust in a small, clean, used spice jar. Make the bead. Cool it down a little (not enough to crack it), and put it back in the flame until the outside surface is hot. Do not get it molting again or the bead will just get smashed when you put it in the dust. When the surface is hot, stick it in the jar and spin it around. Do not touch the edges. Bring it out, and heat it in the flame again until the surface gets hot again—and dip again. Then the bead goes back into the heat until the surface gets just hot enough for the pixie dust to stick (not too hot). Finally, the bead is flame annealed. You will have a nice coating all over the bead.

Then at a show in 1995, Karen witnessed a glass bead making demonstration and was amazed.

"I was obsessed with the flame, and I had to know more. I bought books and studied, eventually deriving my own style from their techniques." An initial obstacle was her intimidation of the gases used in lampwork. "I didn't let that stop me! I just knew I needed to learn everything about the gases, torches, gauges, and safety procedures," she says.

Karen strongly recommends that those interested in lampwork first learn the basics through a class, a book, or both. She taught her husband, Bob, the basics of bead making and, in less than a year, he was making and selling his own borosilicate beads of abstract design. In Karen's case, the local propane distributor helped her set up her equipment. Later, she took bead making classes at the Pittsburgh Center for the Arts. Mainly, though, she was self-taught in the beginning.

"Lampworking is technical. There is a lot to learn and it takes time to develop skills and a personal style. I found my consistent style to be donut shapes created with a variety of color and techniques." The bulk of Karen's inspiration for her beads comes from thoughts about everyday life or little fantasies of mind. For example, her "Ancients" series, she says, takes her to an archeological dig site where she is the anthropologist unearthing beads. Her "Beach Bead" series transports her to one of her favorite places of all. "I am on the beach enjoying the sounds of the sea gulls and the sea, feeling the sand between my toes and the sun beating down."

When beginning a new project, Karen often likes to conjure up a theme. "I make my beads in sets," she explains. "It feels more finished to me than one bead, and it tells a story." After Karen has created the base bead, she incorporates a variety of techniques to manipulate the glass. "I use frits, stringers, latticino, pixie dust, twisties, and aventurine to decorate the bead, depending on the movement of the mental picture I have created," she says. "Flowing or curvy lines remind me of nature, while precise lines and dots inspire more abstract pieces."

Color, Karen insists, is the most important part of the bead-making process. She often discovers color combinations in clothing or in magazines. Not every bead set she creates, however, contains bright or vivid colors. Sometimes she will incorporate more diluted color choices and earth tones into a set, such as one she entitled "Earth's Ore." Those beads, she says, were made of green goldstone and ivory glass that "turned out an interesting brown."

Karen's enthusiasm and creative ambition are boundless, as are the multitude of designs she creates. As she journeys through an artistic world not so ordinary, she says her ultimate goal is to be internationally known and highly collectible. "I would love to bead with the best," Karen says, not realizing that she already does. 🌀

Pharaoh is a bead set from Karen Leonardo's "Ancient" series. A black and ivory base is accented with reduction frits, goldstone, silver leaf, and lines and dots of copper and pewter metallic. The beads are shiny, and sport raised bumps for texture. They are made of Moretti glass. Karen's inspiration for this set comes from her love of Greek, Egyptian, and Roman mythology.

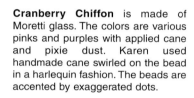

Cranberry Chiffon is made of Moretti glass. The colors are various pinks and purples with applied cane and pixie dust. Karen used handmade cane swirled on the bead in a harlequin fashion. The beads are accented by exaggerated dots.

This **Malibu** bead set is part of Karen's "Beach Beads" series. The colors are tropical with various types of latticino, twisties, lines, dots, frits, and feathering techniques. The beads are made of Moretti glass and are etched for a soft glow.

These **Golden Scepter** beads are from Karen's "Ancients" series. They are made of transparent topaz and yellow glass with dichroic, reduction frits, enamel, goldstone, and pixie dust accents. Organic amber that has been fossilized and "has incredible inclusions" was Karen's inspiration for this set.

CRANBERRY CHIFFON

Necklace
Lampwork by Karen Leonardo
Design by Susan Ray

Finished Length: 28"

Making a smooth transition from lampwork to other glass beads sometimes is tricky. A few too many beads, or too much color can distract from the work. To accent Karen's beautiful chiffon lampwork without losing focus, seed beads were used as spacers. The "air" created between the beads helps silhouette each choreographed section, moving your eye toward the lampwork each step up the neckline. The vintage crystal cubes provide an important breaking point. Notice how you engage the lampwork just above and below it?

CRANBERRY CHIFFON

How-to:
See Single-strand
Necklaces in Basic How-
to Techniques, page 137.

ETCHED WHITE

Wedding necessities now include bridal jewelry. To meet the challenge, Karen created this lacy white lampwork set.

Necklace
Lampwork by Karen Leonardo
Design by Susan Ray

Finished length: 22"

See another example of the use of these beads on page 101.

Today's bride is custom-making her own jewelry and the jewelry for her wedding party. Delicate calligraphy on etched white lampwork and white-on-clear lampwork is the hallmark of this "forever" set of beads. I admit these keepsake beads are better than diamonds. To show off the perfect form and simple elegance of these beautiful beads, silver lined crystal-clear seed beads and copper lined 6/0s easily keep this necklace understated for a walk down any aisle.

Supplies Needed

- Pewter, antique silver finish, toggle
- 2 crimp beads
- 26" flexible wire
- 15 graduated bridal lampwork beads, 9mm to 16mm
- Handful of copper lined 6/0 beads
- Strand of crystal-clear, silver-lined 11/0 seed beads
- 2 sterling silver balls (ending each length just before the crimp bead)

ETCHED WHITE

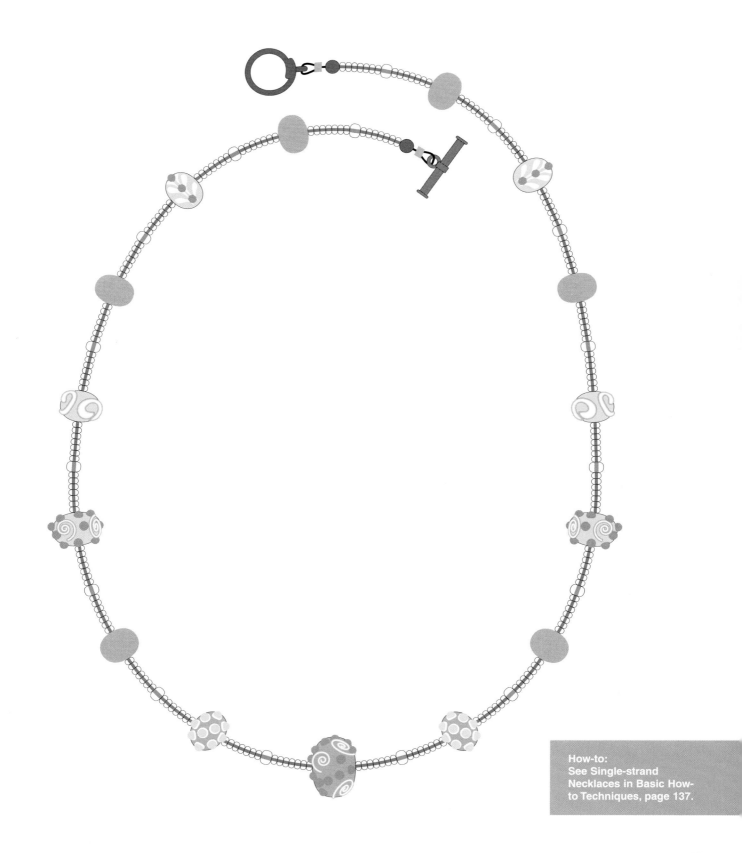

How-to:
See Single-strand
Necklaces in Basic How-
to Techniques, page 137.

ALASKAN
WHARF

Necklace
Lampwork by Tamara Knight
Design by Susan Ray

I did not wake up one day and decide I wanted to become a lamp worker rather it evolved over time out of a basic desire for beads and an innate love of glass.

—Tamara Knight

Tamara Knight is an avowed "beadaholic" whose foray into the medium of glass some twelve years ago has culminated in a level of expertise unmatched by but a few top-notch bead makers. "I take pride in providing a variety of quality beads. Some I consider 'classic' editions with good traditional color groups. Others are 'artist's' beads that have more inspired color combinations, style, and shape." The latter, she says, turn out to be "one-of-a-kind creations."

Born in the state of Washington, Tamara has lived on a ranch in Montana, attended college in Hawaii, and spent several years in Bettles, Alaska (150 miles north of the Arctic Circle), and in Fairbanks where she met her husband. Throughout her travels, Tamara has never stopped making beads. There aren't many bead stores in Alaska, so Tamara's efforts were mainly for her own use and enjoyment.

Tamara now lives in Illinois with her husband Roland and four growing boys. Her artistic flair has flowed into numerous other media including metalsmithing, enameling, ceramics, and woodcarving. Even when she was a young girl, there was no medium that was off limits.

"I was the kind of kid who took nuts and washers and painted them with fingernail polish. Fishing tackle, marbles, and copper tubes were all up for grabs at our house," she says. But in the end, she always comes back to beads, which have remained her primary form of artistic expression.

"I just love the way molten glass flows, so I only make beads now," says Tamara, who relies on a wide variety of glass to obtain her unique colors and effects. Many of her sets will contain beads of more than one type of glass. Tamara's beads may contain Moretti and murano glass from Italy, lauscha glass from Germany, soda glass and lead crystal from the Czech Republic, satake from Japan, and borosilicate made in the United States. She also uses silver and gold, enamels, and specialty techniques like acid etching and sandblasting to produce her varied effects and colors. Tamara is also a perfectionist when crafting beads.

"My number one pet peeve with beads has always been bad holes." You will find that each of Tamara's beads has been cleaned, the hole rims are sanded smooth, and washed to remove any residue. If called for, Tamara uses a marble mold for making sized beads of precise roundness. "Free form" beads, which are made without a mold, are more graduated in appearance. All beads are kiln annealed for lasting strength and durability.

ARTIST'S CONTACT INFORMATION

Tamara A. Knight
Knight Beads
32 Windwood Dr.
Aurora, IL 60506
(630) 466 0979
E-mail: Knightbeads@aol.com
eBay user ID: Knightbeads
Tamara's beads are also available at
Bubbles, Bangles, and Beads,
234 N. Main St.
Galena, IL 61036
(815) 777-9311
Contact Susan Ray at
raysa@www.bubblesbanglesbeads.com

Not only are beads art, but they have a tactile comfort. I wear most beads on an exchange pendant. I often find myself holding the pendant and rubbing it with my fingers. I find it both relaxing and pacifying. When I do not have time to make beads I will just sit and sketch ideas, or sort through my private collection.

—Tamara Knight

"In Hawaii, I spent hours drilling holes on coral, soft rocks, and a variety of local nuts to use as beads," she recalls. Alaskan lore has also been the inspiration for numerous sets of beads.

It was not until Tamara moved to Illinois and hopped on the Internet that she discovered "there were actually other people making glass beads!" That's when she went from scrap glass to Moretti and bought more professional lampworking equipment.

"Almost overnight, I found I was able to accomplish what my mind and instinct called for," she says of the new inspiration and materials.

The world of online bead making provided new impetus for Tamara. "There was a lot of information I had never seen, and people to discuss problems with, especially on the ISGB (International Society of Glass Beads) forum. It was like a whole world opening up finding other artists making beads."

Looking back on the beginnings of her thriving career as a lampworker, Tamara stresses that it was not a sudden, single event that propelled her into the medium. "I did not wake up one day and decide that I wanted to become a lampworker; it evolved over time out of a basic need and desire for beads, and an innate love for glass."

Now approaching the peak of her career, Tamara has time to enjoy her art and craft in a personal way. "I have a little box of beads, my personal little hoard that I have gathered or made over the years," she says. "They will probably never make it into a necklace or anything. I am just happy to take them out to touch them, hold them, and admire their beauty."

Tamara's life is busy with husband Roland, four boys, and a career. When asked what she does to relax, she confesses that she will "often sit and sketch ideas, or sort through my private collection." It's difficult to get away from an art form if you love it the way she does. You can find Tamara discussing lampworking on the ISGB forum (http://www. ISGB.org). 🌑

Blues Set. "These beads began as two sets but were later combined as one. The enamel beads have color depth and half of the turquoise beads have been etched to a matte finish to compliment the glossy surface of the others," says artist Tamara Knight. They are made with Moretti glass and enamels.

Horse Beads. "As a horse owner I enjoy a variety of horse-related activities. I usually create my horse beads from a photo, trying to capture the markings, style, and even the personality of the horse in the beads." They are made of Moretti glass.

"Some cultures believe those who envy you can cause you harm," says Tamara explaining the origin of **Eye Beads**. "The evil eye bead is thought to ward off such negative vibrations. In Turkey, Evil-eye (Nazar) is thought to protect you against bad luck. Almost every house in Turkey has at least one evil-eye ornament, often constructed of several eye beads."

Alaska Set. "I lived in Alaska for several years, not far from a small Inuit Village. In this set, I try to capture the colors and raw artistic flair of the native craft work and rough Alaskan surroundings." The Alaska set was made with Moretti glass.

ALASKAN WHARF

I can recall the Inuit village by my home in Alaska. The beads are rough, raw, and have an appearance of native hand craftsmanship.

—Tamara A. Knight

Finished length: 32", 28", and 26"

Necklace
Lampwork by Tamara Knight
Design by Susan Ray

Tamara is a storyteller. Her beads talk about her travels and the places where she has lived over the years. To complete the story, I added elements that suggest the rugged life style of the Alaskan coast. I asked Tamara to spend a day shopping for beads that would best represent her recollections of her travels. The fetish and the copper nuggets were the first elements that we found. Natural stone quartz, jasper, and aventurine also helped to create the necklace. It is one of my favorite pieces.

TIP: When wrapping sterling wire to form a secure tie for an object you wish to string, start by creating a loop one third larger than the bead requires. Then place the loop around the object and turn it into a simple figure eight. Twist, creating a hanger for the bead. You can make sure the wire is tightly wrapped about the bead and the upper portion of the figure eight acts as the hanging wire.

Supplies Needed

- Sterling silver toggle clasp
- 6 crimp beads
- 98" flexible wire
- 18 Moretti glass Alaskan beads
- Natural stone fetish
- 18 howlite beads, 6mm
- 124 glass discs, 4mm
- 2 copper dust beads
- 24 hematite round beads, 4mm
- 8 natural stone beads up to 18mm x 12mm
- 36" of sterling silver wire in .21 gauge (for wrapping the fetish)
- 2 sterling silver bali spacers
- Assorted seed beads 11/0 and 13/0 in a complimentary mix of colors
- 6 sterling silver balls (ending each length just before the crimp bead)

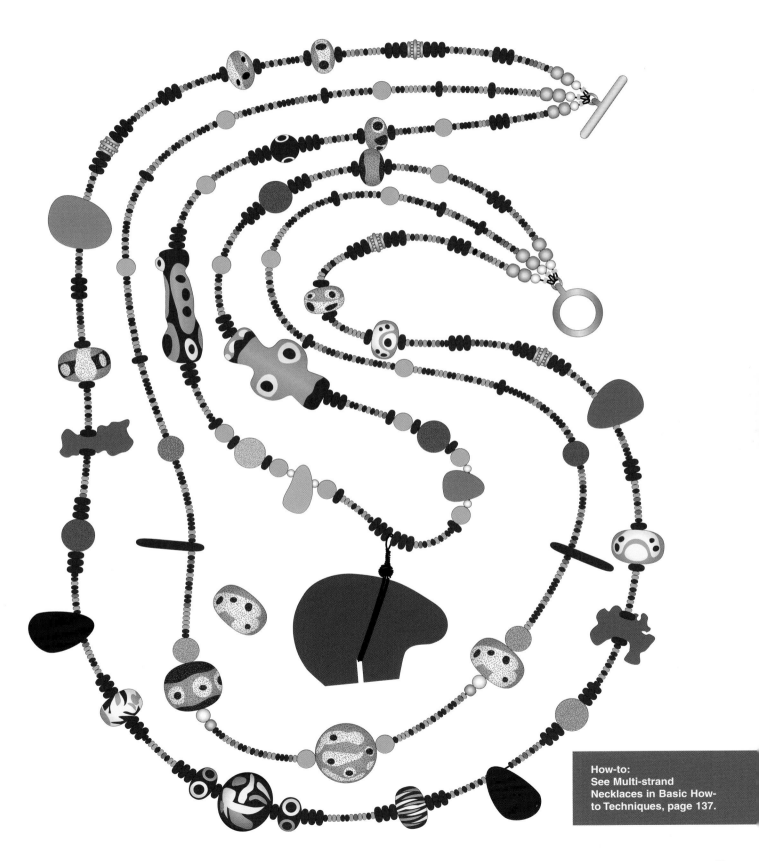

How-to:
See Multi-strand
Necklaces in Basic How-
to Techniques, page 137.

KNIGHT EXEMPLAR

As a horse owner, I create my horse beads from photos to try to captivate the markings, style, and even the personality of the horse.

—Tamara A. Knight

Finished length: 17"

Necklace
Lampwork by Tamara Knight
Design by Susan Ray

The saddle brown amber oval beads were the perfect addition to Tamara's lampwork. The decision to reverse the toggle lent an air of contemporary design and clearly focused the eye on the beautiful horse head and hand wound beads.

Supplies Needed

TIP: Make the beaded necklace first. Attach the bollo chain to the lobster claw ring and the spring ring closure. Make each of the head pin drops attaching each to the small 2-1/2" chain as you go. Then attach the chain with drops to the spring ring end of the lobster claw ring and spring ring closure.

- Lobster claw clasp and spring ring
- 2 crimp beads
- 21" flexible wire
- Moretti glass horse head bead
- 10 coordinating Moretti glass lampwork beads, from 7mm to 14mm
- 23 black glass beads, 5mm
- 30 saddle brown glass or amber beads, 8mm x 6mm
- 9 sterling silver spacer beads, 4mm x 6mm
- 6 head pins
- Eye pin

TIP: the horse head is placed on an eye pin and the lampwork drop is then added to the bottom.

- Silver bollo chain, 16-3/4" in length
- Silver bollo chain, 2-1/2" in length
- 2 sterling silver balls (ending each length just before the crimp bead)
- 2 hand hammered pewter charms, 20mm and 16mm
- 2 pewter jump rings, 15mm and 9mm (to attach charms)

KNIGHT EXEMPLAR

Tamara's exposure to the geographical and cultural extremes of the Pacific Northwest, northern Alaska, Montana, and Hawaii has imparted a unique flavor to her work.

How-to:
See Multi-strand Necklaces in Basic How-to Techniques, page 137.

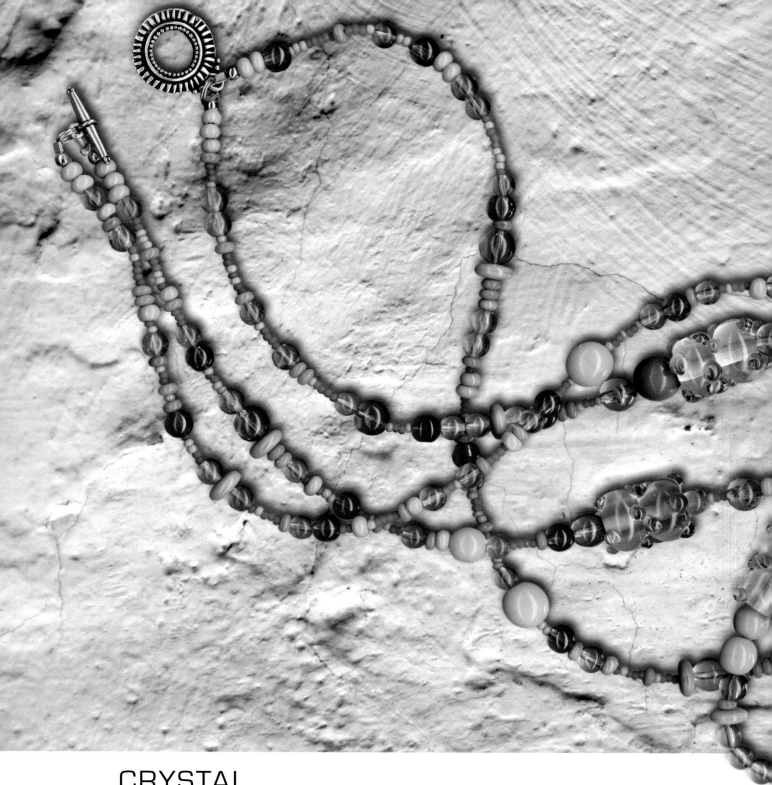

CRYSTAL
PALACE

Necklace
Lampwork by Gary Haun
Design by Sue Wilke

Among his duties as an emergency medical technician at a local drag strip, a volunteer fireman, and a ham radio operator who chases storms for the National Weather Service (not to mention a full-time job), Gary Haun somehow still finds time to craft glass beads of fetching clarity and compelling, yet simple, design. He is a lampwork artist who combines simplicity with precision to conjure up beads that are a treat for the eye and a breeze to work into original jewelry designs. It's nearly impossible to go wrong when stringing a necklace or bracelet with a set of Gary's beads.

It's hard to believe that Gary has been lampworking for only a few years, and what's more, that he does it all in his spare time.

"The first time I saw a glass lampworker was at Disney World in Orlando, Florida," says Gary, reflecting on his introduction to the art of glass bead making. "It was amazing how he heated the glass to a molten flowing stage and made animals, castles, and other figures." As mesmerizing as that initial experience was for him, Gary didn't immediately follow up on lampworking and, in fact, didn't have any contact with lampworking again until he moved from Florida to Lawrenceburg, Tennessee, more than twenty-five years later! There, he once again stumbled upon a lampworker exhibiting his skills, this time at a Christmas fair at a local shopping center.

"I could easily have stood there and watched him for hours," says Gary. However, Gary still did not think of pursuing bead making as a craft that he could master. Indeed, not until the following Christmas, when the same lampworker returned to the local mall, did he begin to ask questions that would finally put him on the path to becoming a professional lampworker.

After getting some practical tips from the touring lampworker, Gary bought a torch, some borosilicate glass, and a couple of Lewis C. Wilson videos. "I was at long last melting glass."

"I made some neat little things but was still having some problems controlling the glass," recalls Gary. "After a couple of phone calls to Lewis Wilson, I was convinced to try Moretti glass which is a soft glass and has a lower melting point than borosilicate glass." Gary bought an assortment of Moretti glass and soon fell in love with the many color combinations he found at his disposal. Up to that point, Gary was entirely self-taught and

ARTIST'S CONTACT INFORMATION

Gary T. Haun
Glass Glass Glass
1650 Little Fishtrap Rd.
Lawrenceburg, TN 38464
(931) 722-9164
E-mail: garyh@netease.net
eBay user ID: glassglassglass

After getting some practical tips from the touring lampworker, Gary bought a torch, some borosilicate glass, and a couple of Lewis C. Wilson videos.

I was at long last melting glass.

—Gary Haun

producing satisfactory but not extraordinary work. However, he says that a two-day lampworking class taken from Deanna Griffin Dove in 2001 changed that.

"Just seeing how she made beads and her instruction really made all the difference in what I could do." Gary has been making beads for about five years now, all in his spare time and all in his basement studio. He concedes that living in a rural area means that there is not a large local market for his work. So, to get that wider audience, he, like many other bead makers, relies on eBay and other Internet venues to find buyers.

Gary now crafts his beads using a Carlisle CC burner torch and "a room full of beautifully colored glass." The results are fine, pure, and simple. They hold their own in combination with virtually any assortment of accessory beads. Keeping his designs simple may be the key to Gary's obvious success in balancing a full schedule with a prosperous "hobby." A husband, a father of three grown children, and a grandfather of two, Gary admits that finding time to make beads can be a challenge, "but we do manage to find time for the things we really want to do."

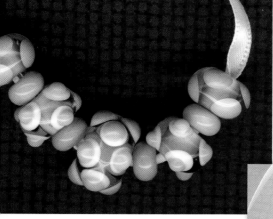

Periwinkle Over Clear. Bead artist Gary Haun's work showcases the value of simplicity of design. Here, periwinkle beads are encased in clear glass, and accented with periwinkle on white dots. The beads are made of Moretti glass. Gary frequently encases pure color with clear glass, allowing the two to capture and reflect light in unexpected ways.

Transparent Raised Dots. This shimmering set is made of green, topaz, or transparent cores with raised dots of transparent blue, green, aqua, and topaz. Gary says he has a special regard for the way transparent colored glass is set off by a clear base. All beads made were made from Moretti glass.

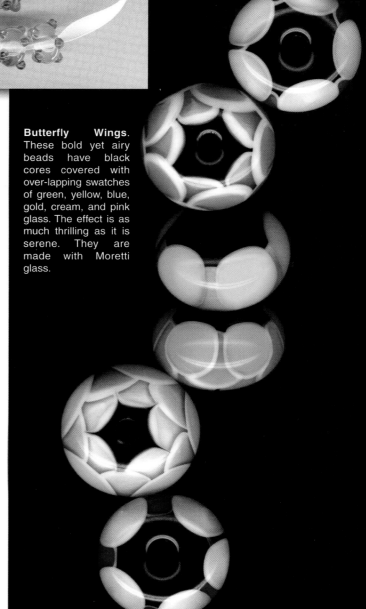

Butterfly Wings. These bold yet airy beads have black cores covered with over-lapping swatches of green, yellow, blue, gold, cream, and pink glass. The effect is as much thrilling as it is serene. They are made with Moretti glass.

Nothing is more assured than the classic look of black-on-white. Gary has it down to perfection in this **Black and White** set where the base colors switch places with the decorative embellishments of dots and spots. Spacer beads are either pure black or pure white, while end beads are spattered with pixie dust for sparkle. All beads are made of Moretti glass.

CRYSTAL PALACE

I really appreciate the way transparent colored glass is set off by a clear glass base.

—Gary Haun

Finished length: 25" and 23"

Necklace
Lampwork by Gary Haun
Design by Sue Wilke

Florence, Italy, comes to mind when the vibrant colors of blue, green, aqua, and topaz are set against a clear glass core. The bold Moretti glass beads seem to just shimmer with inner light. To keep the necklace light and airy, transparent and opaque druks play a major role throughout. The large 16mm x 10mm oval "bumpies" surprise the eye. Best captured by bright daylight, this melody of beads just sings.

TIP: A large mix of complimentary accent beads is placed in a bowl. The beads are then strung in a random order. The large Moretti glass lampwork beads are kept at the same distance adding some symmetry. Although the necklace appears to be completely symmetric, it is not. This adds another element of surprise!

Supplies Needed

- Gold toggle clasp
- 2 crimp beads
- 2 spring rings, 6mm
- 56" flexible wire
- 12 Moretti glass beads, 16mm x 10mm
- Handful of 13/0 opaque, matte seed beads
- Assorted opaque and transparent druks, discs, and other glass beads, 4mm to 8mm
- 2 gold plate balls (ending each length just before the crimp bead), 4mm

How-to:
See Multi-strand Necklace
in Basic How-to
Techniques, page 137.

DRIFTING CLOUDS

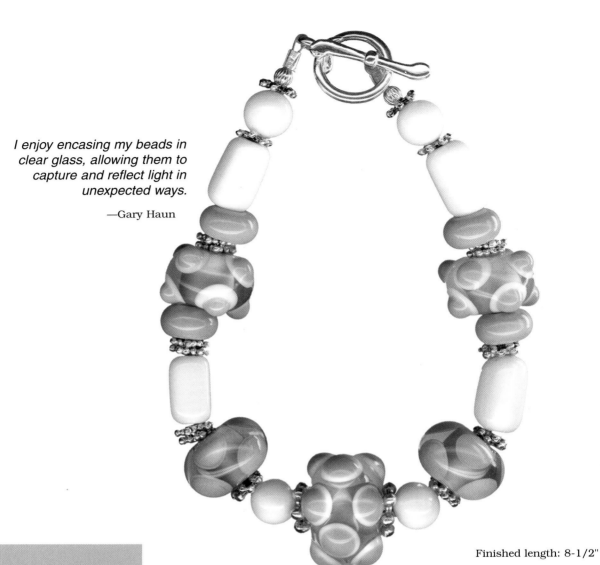

I enjoy encasing my beads in clear glass, allowing them to capture and reflect light in unexpected ways.

—Gary Haun

Necklace
Lampwork by Gary Haun
Design by Mary Beth Sprengelmeyer

Finished length: 8-1/2"

(Remember that large lampwork beads add to the dimension of the bracelet. They often require additional length to make up for the increase in depth.)

The periwinkle hues of Gary's lampwork beads are accented by a tiny edging of white. At first, the challenge of finding an accent bead seemed like it would be easy. But it took several trips to favorite antique haunts to come up with just the right white glass beads to keep this project simple yet elegant. Small sterling silver spacers help to keep the use of light and reflection moving throughout the piece. It takes a camera expert's eye to make such a beautiful, yet subtle bracelet. Thanks, Mary Beth!

Supplies Needed

- Sterling silver toggle closure
- 2 crimp beads
- 12" flexible wire
- 5 periwinkle Moretti glass beads
- 4 Moretti glass opaque periwinkle companion beads, 8mm
- 4 vintage white porcelain rectangles, 9mm x 7mm
- 4 vintage white porcelain round beads, 6mm
- 14 sterling silver bali single and double spacers, 4mm to 7mm
- 2 sterling silver corrugated balls (ending each length just before the crimp bead)

DRIFTING CLOUDS

Glass beads are often decorated with intricate mosaic patterns called millefiori, or "thousand flowers." The effect is achieved by slicing through bundles of differently colored glass rods that have been fused and pulled as one. The cross sectional patterns are then applied to the bead's surface.

How-to:
See Single-strand
Bracelet in Basic How-to
Techniques, page 134.

A BIRD IN HAND

Eyeglasses Holder
Lampwork by Jill Shank
Design by Susan Ray

You can create anything out of a Italian Moretti glass rod. If you're not afraid of it, you can do anything you want once it's molten.

—Jill Lane Shank

Jill Lane Shank has long adored both art and nature, so it is not surprising that she has combined the two into the busy business of crafting specialty beads depicting the insects, birds, and small animals she sees around her studio in Claremore, Oklahoma.

Jill has explored a variety of art forms throughout her life. In addition to taking art classes at public schools, she also studied privately at the Philbrook Museum of Art, where she concentrated on enamel work, pottery, and mixed media. She studied painting under Oklahoma artist Clarence Canning Allen. As she grew older, Jill's artistic interests expanded to photography, silk screening, and stained glass.

"I've always done artwork in some shape or form," recounts Jill. "I just had to have some project going all the time."

Jill began college as an art major with an emphasis on drawing and painting. She planned to be an art teacher until marriage intervened and she eventually settled on a career in nursing, one she continues to this day as a busy home health nurse. During nearly 20 years in nursing, she has worked in obstetric and cardiac units. Jill's medical career is balanced by her duties at home as a mother of three teenage children. Despite demands on her professional and home life, Jill still managed to act on her lifelong love of art.

Jill discovered her love of bead craft while on a family vacation to Asheville, North Carolina, two years ago. After browsing through a bead store there, she signed up for a wire-working course. She decided to continue learning about beads and signed up for a bracelet-making course at a bead store in Tulsa, Oklahoma. There, Jill found a small ladybug bead that she used as the focal piece for a garden-themed bracelet. She loved the ladybug bead so much, she decided to learn how to make beads just like it. That quest lead her to Evergreen, Colorado, and renowned bead artist Ginny Sycuro.

"One thing lead to another, and Ginny invited me to her chalet in the mountains for a weekend workshop," explains Jill. "She is a very accomplished bead artist. And, with a Master's in Education, she is an excellent teacher as well."

ARTIST'S CONTACT INFORMATION

Jill Lane Shank
Bluebird Bead Farm
9998 E. 460 Rd.
Claremore, OK 74017
918 342 2101
E-mail: jill@bluebirdbeads.com
Web site: www.bluebirdbeads.com
eBay user ID: bluebirdbeads

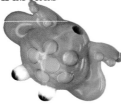

To me, it is very fulfilling to create. At home, working in my bead studio to produce my ladybugs, bluebirds, and bumblebees, I fancifully think of myself as giving life to all the little creatures in my garden. There is also tremendous therapy in creating art. Then, too, when you sell your work, and people get excited about it and smile, it makes you happy, just like the bluebird of happiness!

—Jill Lane Shank

Jill studied lampworking beads for two days with Sycuro, until she could make the ladybug pattern she so treasured from her garden bracelet. Jill also learned to make a bumblebee bead and went home with new inspiration for her craft. Jill left for Tulsa with Sycuro's encouraging words still resonating in her head: "You'll find your niche."

She returned home and, not many months later, launched the Bluebird Bead Farm, a name that reflects Jill's love of the bluebird.

Nature provides an endless source of inspiration for Jill's bead craft. From her sunroom studio overlooking the family's backyard in the country, Jill can gaze out at swooping birds, streams of bees and butterflies, and other fanciful creatures.

Jill says she enjoys lampworking because glass is so versatile. "You can create anything out of an Italian Moretti glass rod. If you're not afraid of it, you can do anything you want once it's molten."

Jill begins by making the base bead then adds more specialized parts for shape and detail (such as the tail of a goldfinch or wings of a dragonfly). She then uses stringers to place the final details, such as the eyes or beak. "If I'm in my studio all day making beads, I can fill the kiln with 50 beads; that's a pretty good day's work. Then I'll spend another couple of hours assembling them, if they are going onto bracelets or necklaces. I use wire working techniques to shape special accessories, like flowers for the jewelry pieces."

Jill's Bluebird Bead Farm has grown rapidly from her first collection of ladybugs, bluebirds, and bumblebees. She now produces eight birds: Goldfinches, bluebirds, blue jays, cardinals, orioles, purple martins, doves, and robins. She also enjoys making insects like the dragonfly, bumblebee, and ladybug. Naturally, flowers populate many of her sets and jewelry pieces. Recently, she began using brighter colors and patterns to make a "groovy" retro theme variation on her standard designs. Themes include Tea Time, Frog on the Lily Pad, Mozart's Music, Flower Power, Field of Daisies, Fun Beads, Pretty in Pink, Seven Seas, Mardi gras, St. Patrick's, and Valentine's Day. She sells beads separately and in sets so customers can have fun making their own jewelry, or as completed pieces ready to wear.

Jill offers private lessons in her studio, and also teaches jewelry creation and design at Ivy Cottage in Claremore, Oklahoma.

"The neatest thing of all," Jill says, "is that my family enjoys my beading as much as I do." Her husband, Tom, helps with marketing while son Ryan handles the computer, uploading digital images to a Web site he created. Daughter Rachel helps her mom assemble jewelry pieces, and Jill's youngest son, John, 12, is "the manager and only employee in the packaging and shipping department." John also is the apprentice beader, learning the trade from Jill. He recently joined his mom for a class taught by Ginny Sycuro. Could this be the start of a glass bead dynasty on the Bluebird Bead Farm?

Whimsical birds, bugs, frogs, and bumblebees are just some of the backyard denizens immortalized in Moretti glass by Jill Shank, "The Queen-Beader" at the Bluebird Bead Farm. Below is a nest full of **Groovy Ladybugs** decked out in viscous retro colors. Right is Jill's favorite subject, the **Bluebird of Happiness.**

A couple of more traditional **Ladybugs** scout their surroundings (left) while a **Bumblebee** stretches its wings.

Jill is ready for all seasons with brilliant designs are just the thing for that special keepsake pendant, brooch, or bracelet. Her **Heart, Pumpkin, Turkey, Christmas Tree, Valentine,** and **Snowman** beads are made with Moretti glass and are kiln annealed.

A BIRD IN HAND

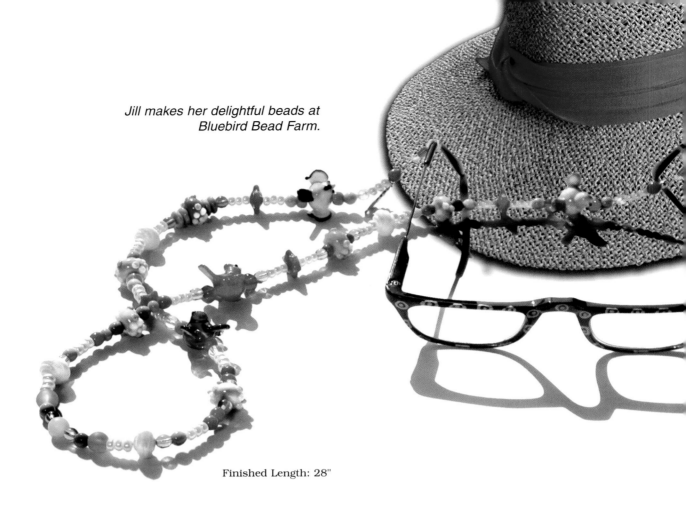

Jill makes her delightful beads at Bluebird Bead Farm.

Finished Length: 28"

Eyeglasses Holder
Lampwork by Jill Lane Shank
Design by Susan Ray

Jill's whimsical Moretti glass birds and floral beads just had to become adorable eyeglass holders. "Glasses always make me look so serious! This was sure to lighten up that 'all business' demeanor. Finding some small red vintage stars and white focal flowers added even more dimension and plenty of smiles. Then stringing varying crow, pearl finish glass beads, and druks together completed this lovely project."

Supplies Needed

- 2 clear eyeglass holders
- 2 crimp beads
- 32" flexible wire
- 4 Moretti glass birds
- 6 Moretti glass floral beads, 12mm
- 4 vintage red star beads, 12mm
- 4 vintage white porcelain flowers, 10mm to 12mm
- Assorted druks, glass pearls, discs, bicone crystals 4mm – 8 mm and color lined rectangles 5mm x 3 mm
- 2 sterling silver balls (ending each length just before the crimp bead)

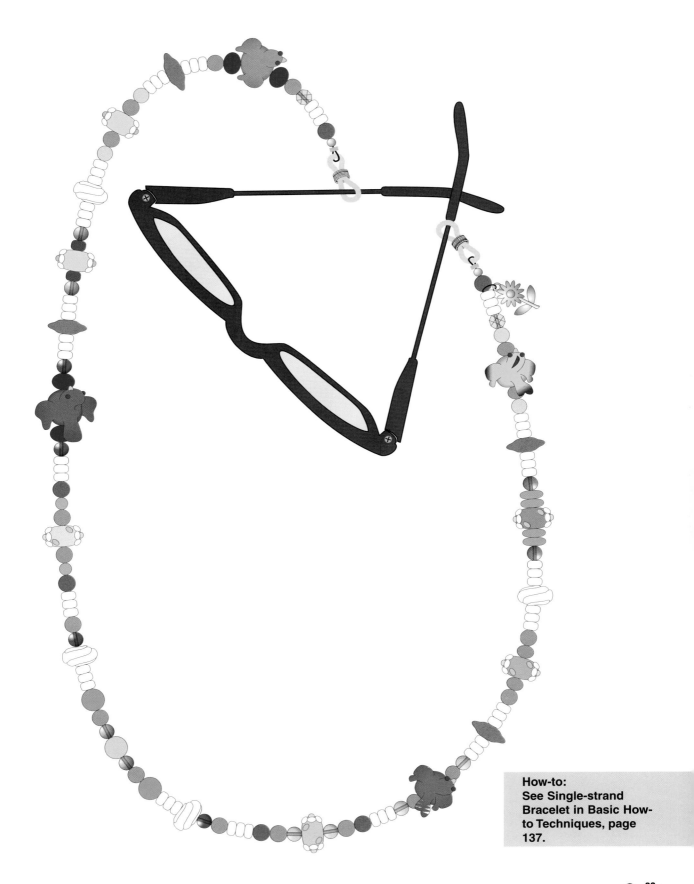

How-to:
See Single-strand
Bracelet in Basic How-
to Techniques, page
137.

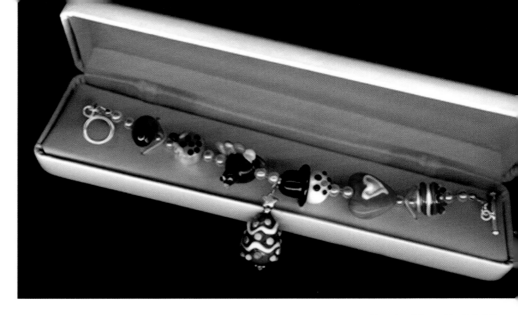

Finished Length: 8-1/2"

Charm Bracelet
Lampwork by Jill Lane Shank
Design by Susan Ray with Angie
Hudek and Rachel Davis

Holidays teach children to count

down the days of the year. This

lampwork bracelet will be a

cheery reminder of time

marching on.

- Patriotic lampwork bead, 10mm
- Little lady bug lampwork bead,
  10mm x 22mm
- Red and white heart lampwork bead
- Snowman lampwork bead, 18mm x
  16mm
- Turkey lampwork bead, 20mm x
  16mm
- Pumpkin lampwork bead, 10mm x
  12mm
- Christmas tree lampwork bead,
  16mm x 24mm

- 14 glass pearls, 4mm to 5mm
- 7 true-cut seed beads, bright orange
- 7 large lampwork holiday beads
- 12" flexible wire
- Sterling silver toggle clasp
- Sterling silver star, 6mm to 7mm
- 4" head pin
- Sterling silver spacer
- 3 sterling silver beads, 2mm to 3mm

TIP: Make up the Christmas Tree Lampwork pendant first. String one sterling silver spacer, Christmas Tree Lampwork, and one sterling silver round ball onto the headpin. Make rosary turn. Clip excess wire away. Set aside. String one half of the beads for the bracelet and then string the pendant where desired. Complete by stringing remaining beads.

TIP: You will need to compensate for the extra large lampwork in the bracelet, so your overall length will end up larger than usual.

FOR ALL SEASONS

One of the oldest pieces of glass in existence today is a single small bead in the Ashmolean Museum in Oxford. It bears the cartouche of the Pharaoh Amenhotep who lived from 1551 to 1527 B.C.

How-to: See Single Strand Bracelet in Basic How-to Techniques, page 134; See Rosary Turn in Basic How-to Techniques, page 138.

TEA TIME

Bracelet
Lampwork by Leigh Funk
Design by Susan Ray

Lampworking has opened up creativity that I didn't even know I had.

—Leigh Funk

Like many of the successful glass artists in this book, Leigh Ann Funk stumbled upon the medium by accident. After dabbling in crochet and counted cross-stitch, she moved to stained glass and then on to lampwork after discovering a book on how to make glass beads in the local stained glass supply store where she was working at the time.

"That was an epiphany for me. I was blown away by the unbelievable colors and shapes, and I knew I was hooked for life," says Leigh of the singular event that launched her prosperous hobby in bead making with an emphasis on turning everyday objects, like milk bottles, ice cream cones, and teapots, into wearable art. Leigh says that she has never really been drawn to finished jewelry, but that the combination of color and form made the process of bead making itself irresistible.

Soon, she was scrutinizing beads wherever she saw them and was sharing some of her finds with her boss at the stained glass shop. Taking the cue, her boss purchased Leigh a torch, and encouraged her to begin exploring the vast world of bead design and lampwork. In addition to the allure of color and design, the actual process of making beads immediately enchanted Leigh.

"Watching the glass melt, forming it, putting one color together with another, then another, then adding layers—I could lose hours making beads." Soon, she wasn't content just to make beads at work. She bought her own torch and began making them at home.

At first, the simple shapes combined with dots or swirls were enough to hold her interest, but she soon found that it was the more complex bead that commanded her attention. "I started to challenge myself. 'If I were to make an ice cream cone, how would I go about it?' I would ask

ARTIST'S CONTACT INFORMATION

Leigh Funk
Funky Beads
2708 E. 46th St.
Davenport, IA 52807
(573) 881-5962

**Sources of
Inspiration:**
Homage to Nature
by Paul Stankard

Making Glass Beads
by Cindy Jenkins

myself, and then go try it. Lampworking has opened up creativity that I didn't even know I had."

Leigh says that when she began making beads, she would often dream about an idea for a bead shape or about various color combinations she wanted to try (and still does to this day). Getting new ideas for beads can come at any time. When she is out of the house, Leigh often carries a small notebook to jot down ideas or draw concepts that may occur to her during the course of the day.

Leigh likes to share her bead making with her husband and three children. She finds them each supportive if not as actively involved in the art as she. (They have all tried it but none has stuck with it.) The children will sit with her as she makes beads, play a favorite CD, or talk about something that happened to them that day. Her husband bought her a new torch for Christmas, and now Leigh jokingly says that she stops only when she runs out of oxygen. In addition to offering classes in her studio, Leigh demonstrates bead making regularly in public, most notably at Columbia's annual "Twilight Festival." She says she particularly enjoys how people will walk by with a vacant expression on their faces, "and then catch sight of the fire and the molten glass and snap to attention. They seem fascinated by the sight," she says, adding that viewers will often ask her to make a turtle, snake, horse, or some other creature. "They are delighted when I show them the finished bead, and I love the togetherness these events afford."

After several years of nearly constant bead making, Leigh found herself with an abundance of beads. "Making jewelry naturally followed," she says. "While I resented this necessity at first, I've begun to enjoy the process now." It has also helped her tailor her bead making toward the ultimate goal: a finished piece of jewelry. Instead of lots of random beads, she now thinks in terms of series of beads.

"Lampworking satisfies my consuming need for color and creativity." 🌀

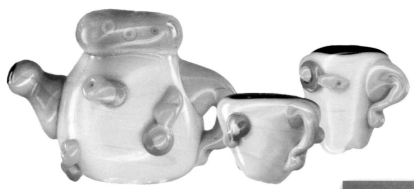

Tea Pot and Cups. All the beads on this page were made with a single-gas bench burner and soft Moretti glass. The cups above have a center of light topaz glass to resemble tea.

Leigh's **Fruit of the Flame** set of formed beads includes oranges, limes, watermelons, grapes, and lemons. They are acid-etched to look frosty and delicious.

These **Kitty, Puppy, and Treats** figure beads are made with a soft Moretti glass for easy manipulation of the molten glass. Shapes come easy to Leigh Funk, who has become an expert at making the formed bead. Leigh says that ideas sometimes come to her in her dreams.

Friendly Fowls appear perplexed; the placement of the eyes give these birds of a feather a decidedly comical look.

"The ideas come to me in my dreams," says Leigh. Sweet dreams, Leigh. They must be very sweet dreams too!

Finished Length: 7" bracelet or 10 " ankle bracelet

Bracelet
Lampwork by Leigh Funk
Design by Susan Ray

Sweet and innocent: This tiny tea service in Moretti glass brings back memories of a gentle time when I played dress-up and spent the afternoons sharing muffins and tea with my teddy bears. The blue sky teapot, and sugar and creamer are highlighted with color lined rectangle beads, round and bicone crystals. The sterling stars and clasp add silvery accents.

- 6 crimp beads
- Sterling silver toggle clasp
- 2 sterling silver stars, 11mm
- 3 pieces of 12" flexible wire (for bracelet) or 3 pieces of 14" flexible wire (for ankle bracelet)
- 3 Moretti lampwork beads (Teapot, Sugar, and Creamer)
- 16 to 24 assorted bicone and round faceted crystals 4mm to 8 mm
- 6 sterling silver balls (ending each length just before the crimp bead)
- 1 strand 11/0 or 13/0 seed beads
- Assorted color-lined rectangles, 5mm x 3 mm

TEA TIME

The art of forging decorative glass beads from a mixture of sand and soda heated with lime dates back to at least 2500 B.C. in Mesopotamia. Glass making became very popular with ancient Egyptians but was technically perfected by the Romans and, later, the Venetians who to this day remain preeminent glass artisans. Glassmakers have traditionally kept essential techniques and ingredients a secret, passing them down only by word of mouth. This, too, remains a custom to the present day.

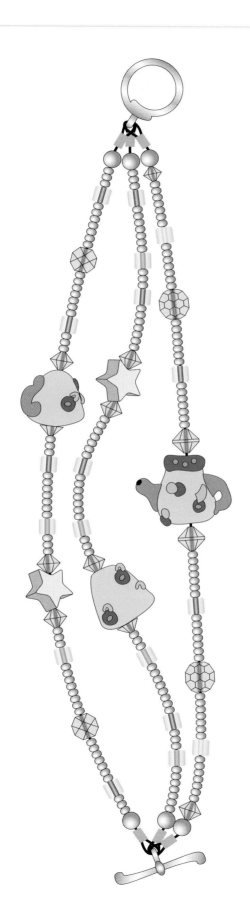

How-to:
See Multi-Strand
Bracelets
 in Basic How-to
Techniques, page 136.

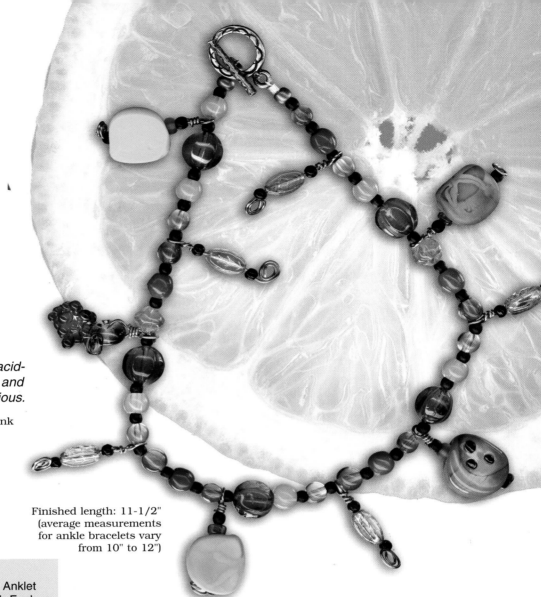

TUTTI FRUITY

The fruit lampwork is acid-etched to look frosty and delicious.

—Leigh Funk

Finished length: 11-1/2"
(average measurements
for ankle bracelets vary
from 10" to 12")

Anklet
Lampwork by Leigh Funk
Design by Susan Ray

These tiny Moretti fruits, in such

brilliant colors, conjure up Miami

nightlife and Carmen Miranda. We

couldn't help indulging our senses!

- Copper toggle clasp
- 2 crimp beads
- 16" flexible wire
- 5 Moretti glass fruits
- 1-1/2 feet of copper wire (to hand make eye pin drops)
- 5 transparent glass ovals 8mm x 6mm
- Assorted druks and glass beads (transparent and opaque), 5mm to 10mm
- 4 dozen black glass beads, 2mm
- 2 copper balls (ending each length just before the crimp bead)

Supplies Needed

TIP: *Make the ten fruit and oval bead rosary turn drops prior to stringing your ankle bracelet. Then you can string the drops as you go. Make a turned "eye" to act as a bead stop.*

TIP: *Stringing one tiny 2mm black bead between the brightly colored beads and drops creatively ties the assortment together.*

How-to: See Single-strand
Bracelet in Basic How-to
Techniques, page 134; See
Rosary Turns in Basic How-to
Techniques, page 138.

CHA CHA BRACELET

Bracelet
Lampwork by Lynn Nurge
Design by Brittany Berndston and Susan Ray

One of the sweetest parts of bead making is opening the kiln and seeing that one bead that just makes you smile from the inside out.

—Lynn Nurge

Lynn Nurge has enjoyed a life surrounded by glass beads and gemstones. As a child, she used to play with her grandmother's pearls and her aunt's large jewelry pieces while her mother was a superb seamstress, who sewed clothes with delicate ruffles and seed beads. Lynn has fond memories of the latter, recalling both her majorette costumes that were covered in pearls and beads with a touch of rhinestones for sparkle, and a prom dress that was the envy of her classmates. "I was 'imprinted' by beads at an early age," she says of those formative years. But she was soon to move into the realm of gemstones, jewelry making, and ultimately lampwork for both fun and profit.

Lynn and her husband, Al, a geologist she met in her second year in college, spent their first years together mining minerals and perfecting the art of lapidary jewelry. By the time their first two children were born, they had opened their own custom jewelry store and Lynn had fallen in love with precious and semi-precious beads. The jewelry business gave Lynn the chance to dabble in design using color and texture to create unique bead strands. "Untangling jewelry strands became one of my specialties at the store," she jokes. "I loved ametrine (amethyst and citrine together); this stone was unique and Al found some large pieces of it that I turned into beautiful stones. I would design the mounting—a pendant, bracelet, broach, or earrings—carefully placing the layout of the main stone with its accent stones." Meanwhile, Al carved the wax, cast the piece in precious metals, and set the stones.

Lynn says that she and her husband enjoyed having their own business. For one thing, the kids could join them after school, playing in a small room in the back of the store. After seven years in the lapidary business, though, and with the birth of their third child, they closed the store and began exhibiting at art and craft malls where Lynn sewed chenille animals, painted miniature wood animals, and wire wrapped jewelry. Then, as it does for so many bead artists, serendipity struck when, at one of their favorite gem and mineral shows, an artist making enamel glass beads transfixed Lynn and her husband.

"Those beautiful colors and patterns were little bits of God's handiwork. It never occurred to me at the time that someday I would be able to produce my own little lovelies."

Lynn's husband kept lampworking in mind and later purchased her a borosilicate glass starter set. The idea was to make glass animals that their daughter had begun to collect. But then the husband and wife team began to sell their sculptured glass figurines at art and craft fairs. Except for engraving, Lynn

ARTIST'S CONTACT INFORMATION

Lynn Nurge
Our Favorite Things
407A South Alister, Box 777
Port Aransas, TX 78373
(361) 749-3404
E-mail: lnurge@islandartglass.com
Web site: islandartglass.com
eBay user
ID:
glassmon

Favorite Suppliers for Tools & Glass:
Glass Craft
626 Moss Street
Golden, CO 80401
(888) 272-3830

Arrow Springs
4301 Product Drive
Shingle Springs, CA 95682
(530) 677-1400

Buy for the project intended. Delicate construction may be acceptable for a collectible bead, which will sit safely on a shelf, but very inappropriate for use in a bracelet which will see heavy use. If you like larger or unusually shaped beads (I do!), use of borosilicate glass is a must. It has a much higher degree of strength and workability.

—Lynn Nurge

still had no hands-on with the glass herself. But after recalling her parent's words: "there is nothing you can't do; just get a book, learn, and practice," Lynn started searching for a how-to book on bead making.

"In June of 1998 I found a beginner's book for lampworkers. Al bought me some Moretti glass, and I was on my way."

Lynn began with a single gas butane torch. "This magical little torch, although noisy, is still my favorite over the larger oxygen-propane torches," she says. Lynn rather quickly mastered dot stringers, twists, pokes, pulls, chevrons, millefiori, flowers, and animals. The combination of glass sculptures with beaded jewelry appeared to appeal to their customers. "It seemed we could possibly earn a living this way!" For Lynn, the appeal of the shows was more than commercial however.

"I remember one afternoon a little girl passing our booth stopped suddenly in her tracks when she saw my beads. 'Mommy, how beautiful!' she exclaimed. She couldn't be torn away until she had thoroughly examined every bead on the table with her child's wide-eyed look of pure joy. Later that day, a sweet lady who could not have been younger than eighty years old stopped by and was also fascinated. Her movements were slower, but the expression on her face and the light in her eyes were exactly those of the child. Watching her, I knew that for a few moments she was once again six years old, living in that world where everything is new, and bright, and wonderful. It was the first time I felt that I had truly touched someone through my work."

Lynn, along with her husband and their youngest son, now lives in Port Aransas, Texas, which is on one of the barrier islands outside Corpus Christi. They have opened a glass studio, Our Favorite Things, next to the only ice cream parlor in town. They keep busy demonstrating during store hours and selling their own crop of lampwork sculptures along with Lynn's diamond-point engravings, wire wrappings, bead stringings and, of course, her handsome glass beads.

The online auction house eBay helps fill in business when the tourists are few. Lynn says she makes 8 to 15 bead sets a week to sell on eBay, along with any special orders for jewelry designers or regular patrons. With all that work, it might seem that bead making could grow tiresome ... but not for Lynn, who insists that "one of the sweetest parts of bead making is opening the kiln and seeing that one bead that just makes you smile from the inside out. It's just like a child peeking around the corner at what's under the tree on Christmas." Not that Lynn doesn't seek solace from time to time. "Sometimes I get so busy and caught up crafting a bead that I just have to stop, lock the door, and get away for awhile. A walk on the beach or a short time watching the dolphins play from my favorite rock on the south jetty is usually all it takes to get my mind right again." Lynn says that they are not getting rich, but having a great place to live—on an island inhabited by super people, surrounded by playing dolphins, squawking sea birds, and dancing pelicans—is riches enough. ☻

Soft tones of violet, mauve, and lavender are blended with light earth tones in Lynn Nurge's **Serenity Set.** An occasional touch of black, white, and ochre add contrast and definition. Lynn says that because of the subdued color scheme, she used a mix of internal and external decoration in a variety of patterns "to keep a high level of interest." She has succeeded splendidly, we think.

Keyboard Complexity is a set of black and white Moretti beads that shine like the keys of the piano, yet contrast like notes on a page. Its theme is "counterpoint," the musical term describing the opposition of melodic or rhythmic lines. Black and white provide "infinite combinations and the ultimate contrast so even the most detailed and complex patterns show clearly," says Lynn.

Entrapment is a set of borosilicate beads with a clever central "trapped" bead. The outer beads are made of black cores and thick transparent casings with floating patterns of gold, green, and blue. The focal bead is really two parts: a central, gold-and-green honeycomb borosilicate ball inside a spiral cage made of colorless glass. Lynn says that she loves to work with borosilicate glass because it allows her "to do things that are either impractical or outright impossible with any of the soft glasses."

Watercolor Landscape is a set of nine multicolor cylindrical beads adorned with raised black dots. They are created with a Moretti glass base with applied enamels, frits, and stringers. "These are all about color and texture," says Lynn. "New shades are created wherever individual colors overlap; they blend and mix like in a watercolor landscape."

CHA CHA BRACELET

Keyboard complexity describes this set of black and white Moretti beads that shine like the keys of the piano yet contrast like notes on a page.

—Lynn Nurge

Bracelet
Lampwork by Lynn Nurge
Design by Brittany Berndston

Finished length: Unstretched
inside diameter 2-1/2"

Cha Cha bracelets come in two-row and three-row varieties. We used a two-row bracelet for this project.

Cha Cha bracelets are all the rage, so we just had to include one in our book. How special to use a wonderful matched set of Lynn Nurge's lampwork beads as the focal piece for this fun bracelet! 84 t-pins later, a new "take me dancing" bracelet is born! Brittany tells us she made this project in about an hour with the help of her friend, Meghan Chapman. They packed up supplies and did it in the car on the way to a concert! Cha Cha bracelets (sans beads) are now available through several bead suppliers.

Supplies Needed

- 40 fabulous black-and-white Moretti glass beads, 8mm to 16mm
- Assorted sterling silver balls
- 84 sterling silver head pins
- Assorted shape glass beads, both black and white 2mm to 10 mm

TIP: String all 84 pins and place aside without creating the turns. Vary your patterns, but remember to make some duplicates. The repetition lends continuity to the design. The rosary turns must be made as you go. Start at one end of the bracelet and turn each of the two rows before proceeding.

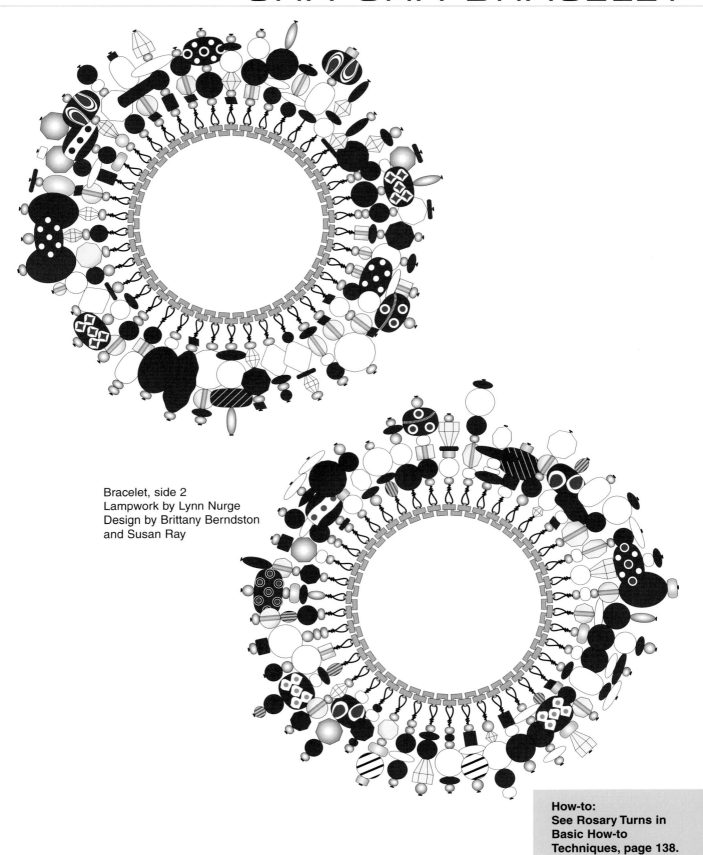

Bracelet, side 2
Lampwork by Lynn Nurge
Design by Brittany Berndston
and Susan Ray

**How-to:
See Rosary Turns in
Basic How-to
Techniques, page 138.**

CHARMED, I'M SURE

This set begins with soft tones of violet, mauve, and lavender. The beads are blended with light earth tones and an occasional touch of black, white, and ochre to add contrast and definition.

—Lynn Nurge

Finished length: 8"

Charm Bracelet
Lampwork by Lynn Nurge
Design by Susan Ray

Supplies Needed

- 27 lampwork beads, 8mm to 12mm
- 22 sterling silver head pins
- Pre-made charm bracelet, 8" length with toggle clasp
- 44 sterling silver round, seamless, or corrugated beads
- Assorted bali silver spacers

TIP: String all of your head pins with beads and set aside. Remember to vary your patterns but allow for some duplicates. This adds consistency to the design. Starting on one end of the bracelet, create the rosary turns right onto the twisted cable links of the bracelet. This bracelet works up so quickly it would be a great gift giver!

TIP: Try on your chain link bracelet to check for proper fit. Varying the size 1/4" to 1/2" can make a lot of difference in comfort.

"Put your purple dress on, we are stepping out!" This bracelet will rock the night away. With just a tiny bit of movement, you come to appreciate the annealing process used to assure your lampwork beads will dance with you for years to come! Lynn is known for making wonderfully large sets of matched lampwork beads to delight any beader. Taking its backbone from the charm bracelets of the '60s, "Charmed, I'm Sure!" gets its textural richness from the indulgence of so many beads to play with.

CHARMED, I'M SURE

Vary your style by alternating beads and charms. A simple spring ring works for attaching charms. Create a theme using like charms. Embellish with beaded head pins.

How-to:
See Rosary Turns in
Basic How-to
Techniques, page 138.

CAT'S MEOW

Bracelet
Lampwork by Amy Caswell
Design by Susan Ray

My husband said, "Just take your sketched cats and make them in 3-D!"

—Amy Caswell

Southern California bead artist Amy Caswell has a cartoonist's eye when it comes to developing new members for her ever-expanding glass menagerie. Her fanciful creations start as pencil drawings inspired by ideas friends and relatives send her, or pictures she sees in books. She never suspected that a childhood penchant for drawing cat figures would evolve into the serious business of making high-quality glass beads that would fetch impressive prices in stores and over the Internet. Amy's childhood doodling has morphed rather quickly into the rewarding artistry of specialty lampwork.

Born in Thousand Oaks, California, Amy Caswell was surrounded by creative people, but as a teenager had no overriding artistic interests of her own. Her mother and grandmother were both oil painters and her sister was a talented ceramist and woodworker. Even her husband, whom she met after graduating from high school, spent much of his free time forging Damascus knives and swords.

"I didn't have a creative side besides sketching 'cartoon-y' cats during math class," says Amy of her teen years. Then one day, years later, she saw a coworker wearing an impressive pair of lampworked earrings. "Every time she wore these earrings I'd be in awe of the colors and style," says Amy. "I went to craft stores in my area but was unable to find anything that looked remotely like those beautiful beads."

Amy's growing interest in beads soon found her stringing simple jewelry pieces to go with "this or that" outfit. The beads she used mostly came from local bead stores, or were scavenged from old jewelry. She did not consider trying to make beads herself until she and her husband visited their local library. While looking through books for jewelry ideas, she showed her husband some impressive lampwork pieces. He said, "I'm sure you could do that!" It wasn't long before Amy had a copy of Cindy Jenkins' Making Glass Beads in hand, a book that she says encouraged her to think that lampworking was within her reach after all.

"I bought some videos, and studied that book," says Amy. "Soon, I bought some very basic supplies and I was on my way."

Amy Caswell

ARTIST'S CONTACT INFORMATION

Amy Caswell
Caswell Studios
173 Ventu Park Road
Newbury Park, CA 91320
(805) 499-0707
E-mail: catlady@caswellian.com
Web site: www.caswellian.com
eBay user ID: acaswell

Favorite Bead Shop:

Creative Castle
2321 Michael Drive
Newbury Park, CA 91320
805 499 1377

At first, Amy limited herself to making simple beads but quickly began adding special art effects. People seemed to like her beads, she says, but she was not completely satisfied. Her husband urged her to concentrate on making "cartoon beads," pointing out that cats and other creatures were what she enjoys and draws most naturally. One day he said to Amy, "Just take your sketched cats and make them in 3-D!"

Amy says her cat beads really started to improve as she began to develop her own style and methods, but she was still unconvinced anyone would pay money for them, and was, by her own admission, terrified to post them on eBay. Eventually she found that courage and offered one for auction. It sold right away and for slightly more than Amy had expected!

Today, one of Amy's greatest challenges is production. Her menagerie has grown to include "Drake the Dragon" and "Feliz the Dog." She can't always make enough beads to keep up with demand and keeping a set posted on eBay is sometimes a real effort. Amy's customers range from cat enthusiasts, breeders, cat owners, people who want a memorial piece of a beloved pet, and anyone who likes whimsical beads.

Reflecting on her still young career, Amy asserts that it has been fun re-creating the kitties that she used to doodle during her earlier years but adds: "The funny thing is, I still haven't tried to re-create the earrings of my coworker. I guess they just weren't my style!"

"One of the reasons I like lampworking is its novelty. The fact is, most jewelry today is mass produced and terribly unimaginative or worse: it's gaudy! I know I'd rather wear something unique and distinctive, one-of-a-kind. Also, unless you're willing to wear something painted or plastic, there isn't a lot of opportunity for color in modern jewelry. Lampwork is a traditional medium offering an unprecedented range of vibrant colors. There's something about a quality glass bead that simply transcends epoxies and plastics. The feel, the heft, the clarity ... the worth of a good glass bead is something that can be both seen and felt." ☻

Hang in There, America. Sculptural patriotic pussycat bead made of Moretti glass. The character was created to express a message of hope for America and to raise money for the United Way and the American Red Cross.

Cliff is another pussycat bead made of Moretti glass. Never without his tuxedo, Cliff is always ready for a party—provided he can find it.

Abe is one of Amy Caswell's "Tuxedo" kitties. Amy is one of those cat lovers who is allergic to the real thing, so these versions, crafted in Moretti glass from her cartoon sketches, allow her to enjoy feline company without the sneezing.

Truffle was inspired by a chocolate-covered fudge confection called "Truffle Hearts." "It's the type of fudge that's moist, rich, and just melts in your mouth," says Amy. Hers is actually made of brown, orange, and cream Moretti glass.

Lola the Leopard is also sculptured of Italian Moretti glass. Lola was inspired by some beautifully patterned round beads Amy saw on the Internet. "I experimented, trying to replicate the pattern, and stumbled upon this spot-making technique in the process!"

Some of Amy's favorite characters are these tiny dragons.

Allergies prevent Amy from having a real cat at home. Her Moretti glass tuxedo cats are a sure-fire replacement and they can go wherever she goes.

CAT'S MEOW

Finished length: 7-1/2"

Charm Bracelet
Lampwork by Amy Caswell
Design by Susan Ray

Supplies Needed

- 7-1/2" sterling silver charm bracelet
- Moretti glass cat bead, 40mm
- Sterling silver cat lover's charm
- 3" sterling silver .21 gauge half-hard head pins, 20
- 15 crystal bicones, 4mm x 8mm to 6mm x 12mm
- Assorted 2mm to 7mm black glass beads
- Assorted silver spacers (even a vintage rhinestone roundel or two)
- 4mm sterling silver balls

TIP: String a bead design you like onto a head pin. And then create a second one just like it. Place them randomly throughout the charm bracelet. Our bracelet is not symmetrical but the repeated patterns do help to tie the bracelet together. Make two copies of several of your designs.

Note: When working with remade bracelet links, you must either turn head pins directly onto each link or use spring rings to attach each head pin.

Everyone remembers a black-and-white cat! Well, everyone who has ever had a black-and-white cat smiles when they see this one. Black-and-white cats just seem to know they are special, mischievous, and charming. They can frighten the daylights out of you by walking around on the roof and then spend the afternoon purring in your lap. When the "I love my cat" charm appeared in a vendor catalog, I knew exactly what this bracelet would look like. I had been hoarding red crystal bicones for months: perfect. Bali silver, crystals, and tiny black glass beads add a lot to the harmony of this bracelet. Now if only he could MEOW. This one is dedicated to my son's very own "Fluffy."

CAT'S MEOW

During the two World Wars of the twentieth century, when their men were away from home, Venetian women supported their families by making tiny glass "seed beads" for worldwide export.

How-to: See Rosary Turns in Basic How-to Techniques page 138; See Single-strand Bracelet in Basic How-to Techniques, page 134.

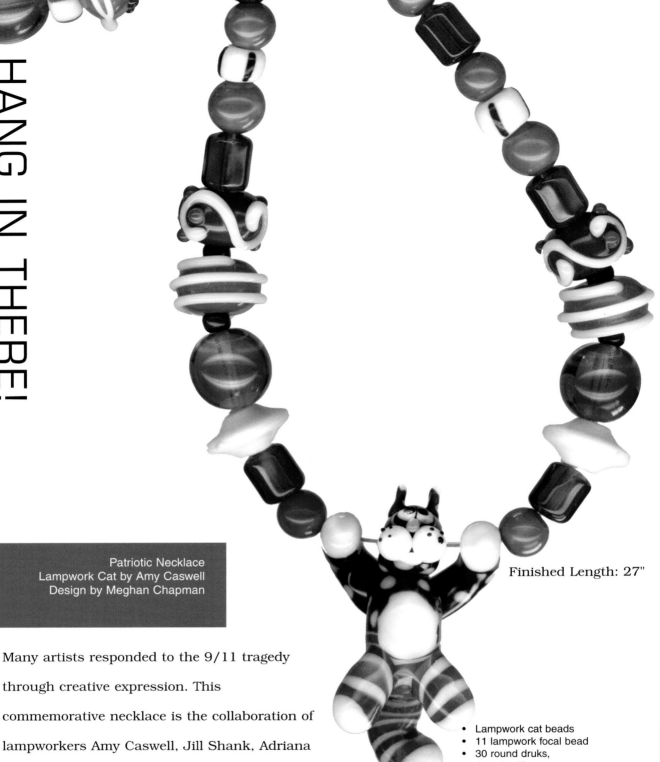

HANG IN THERE!

Patriotic Necklace
Lampwork Cat by Amy Caswell
Design by Meghan Chapman

Finished Length: 27"

Many artists responded to the 9/11 tragedy through creative expression. This commemorative necklace is the collaboration of lampworkers Amy Caswell, Jill Shank, Adriana Sauceda, and Lynn Nurge. This patriotic pussy-cat bead by Amy Caswell expresses hope for America. A portion of the proceeds from patriotic cat beads, like these made by Amy Caswell, goes to raise money for the United Way and the American Red Cross.

Supplies Needed

- Lampwork cat beads
- 11 lampwork focal bead
- 30 round druks,
  4mm to 12mm
- 8 rice beads, 2mm x 4mm
- 14 barrels and teardrops, 3mm x 6mm
- 6 discs, 2mm and 12mm
- 8 striped rounds, 7mm
- 4 striped rounds, 5mm
- 4 white rounds, 10mm
- 4 silver tone squares, 2mm x 4mm
- 2 silver balls, 2mm
- 31" flexible wire
- 2 sterling silver crimp beads
- Lobster claw clasp
- Sterling silver headpin
- 6/0 seed bead for bottom of dangle)

How-to: See Single Strand Necklace in Basic How-to Techniques, page 137; See Rosary Turn in Basic How-to Techniques, page 138.

FLOURISH

Necklace Lariat
Lampwork by Adriana C. Sauceda
Design by Susan Ray

It's wonderful to be able to create such tiny works of art, and to know that what I am wearing reflects my heritage.

—Adriana C.
Sauceda

It was an accident of fate that opened the door to a successful career in bead making for Adriana C. Sauceda. Though creative in many ways as a child and after college as a makeup artist for an international cosmetics firm, Adriana's true calling as a bead artist did not emerge until after she was forced into a part-time position following the abrupt onset of epilepsy. The seizures initially kept her in a low profile, and the big question was: How best to fill up her spare time? While working part-time as an insurance adjuster, Adriana befriended a coworker who, she later discovered, was making jewelry in her free time. Soon, Adriana was stringing jewelry herself but the artistic challenge of putting together other people's beads didn't satisfy her for long.

"After trying my hand at jewelry making for several months, I decided to try crafting my own beads," explains Adriana about her beginnings in the field. A newspaper article on lampwork prompted her to go out and purchase a bead making kit of her own. Classes were available but they were too far from home so it was working from the kit or nothing.

"I never took a single class; I am completely self-taught," she says. Happily, the epilepsy proved manageable with medication, giving Adriana the green light to work with the open flame of a glassblower's torch. She was soon able to quit her part-time job and take up bead making—and motherhood—full time.

Adriana says that her passion for lampwork beads has to do with a desire to "stand out" and be noticed. "I love being unique and having things that other people want—who doesn't?" she says candidly. Her beads certainly do stand out, flaunting the vivid colors of the Southwest with free and bold designs. "I love putting unique designs together, and most of them are bright colors similar to those found in San Antonio, Texas, which tend to reflect our local heritage. It's wonderful to be able to create such tiny works of art, and to know that what I am wearing reflects my heritage and where I'm from."

Adriana C. Sauceda

ARTIST'S CONTACT INFORMATION

Adriana C. Sauceda
Addiebeads/Lampwerks
(210) 240-3528
E-mail: Adriana@lampwerks.com
Web site: www.lampwerks.com
eBay user ID: Addienattie

> *Just as any artist who paints, sculpts, draws, or molds would say that their jobs are professions, the same is true for a glass artist, which is what I consider myself.*
>
> —Adriana C. Sauceda

For inspiration, Adriana draws on her surroundings—both natural and manmade. "I would have to say my main inspiration is nature, as many of my designs are floral. However, another principal source of ideas comes from Fiesta in San Antonio, where many of the bright colors I use are exhibited. They could be at a table in a restaurant, a street vendor, or parade. I've even jotted down the colors from tiling in a bathroom."

Adriana admits that she "caught a lot of flack" for quitting her "real job," but insists that lampworking is a real job, too. "Just as any artist who paints, sculpts, draws, or molds would say that their jobs are professions, the same is true for a glass artist, which is what I consider myself." Her decision to make the career change has paid off. Adriana now sells her creations on a regular basis on eBay (under the user ID Addienattie), at her Web page (www.lampwerks.com), and through retailers and the many repeat customers, which she lauds most of all. Indeed, if anything, Adriana Sauceda may have become too successful. In order to spend more time with her daughter, she now has to limit the number of orders she can accept.

In the end, Adriana says that beads have a special meaning for everyone. "Mine are a constant reminder of how fortunate I am to have been blessed with such a wonderful talent and to be from such a beautiful place. As crazy as it may sound, I owe my bead making abilities and current success to those first seizures! My mom was right when she said "God has a reason for everything." ☻

Night Parade was inspired by "A Night in Old San Antonio," the climax of that town's Fiesta Week. Adriana C. Sauceda says the streamers, confetti, and whirls of color of the festival never fail to delight her, year after year. "I feel that these beads convey the essence of Fiesta in the simplest way possible." The glass is Moretti.

Adriana Sauceda made this **Pink Floral** set to as "a tribute to being feminine." She says that for her, these soft color combinations of pink and lime represent that feeling perfectly. Adriana was so happy with this set that she reserved it exclusively for this book. The beads are made of Moretti glass.

Assorted Brights. "This is my most popular set, and what, I am told, I am most known for—along with my florals," says Adriana. Her inspiration for this cheerful set comes from the colors of San Antonio itself. Fiesta is the chosen theme for quite a few restaurants in town and on the Riverwalk. "It's just a fun set that exudes happiness." The set is made of Moretti glass.

American Floral. This set was inspired by the incidents that occurred in September of 2001. Adriana says that she initially struggled with the idea of doing a tribute. But an e-mail from one of her customers made her realize that people wanted to wear these colors. "There was a strong desire to express our love and dedication to our country ... there was certainly nothing wrong with allowing people to express themselves," she concluded. The set is made of Moretti glass.

FLOURISH

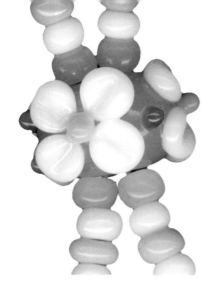

These soft color combinations of pink and lime represent being feminine perfectly.

Finished Length: 57"

Necklace Lariat
Lampwork by Adriana Sauceda
Design by Susan Ray

Supplies Needed

- 62" flexible wire
- Strand of 6/0 of each of the following:
  pink aurora borealis
  pearl white
  lime green
- Handful of copper, 6/0
- 6 bicone crystals 5mm x 10mm to 6mm x 12mm
- Assorted pearls, 4mm to 8mm
- Handful of seed beads
- 5 lampwork beads, 10mm to 15mm
- 2 silver head pins, 4" in length
- 2 vintage faceted crystals, 10mm
- 2 ovals, 8mm x 4mm
- 6 pink druks 6mm
- 2 sterling silver balls (ending each length just before the crimp bead)

TIP: Fill two head pins with beads and make rosary turns. Set aside. Start the lariat by attaching the flexible wire to one of the pre-made head pins. Crimp in place. String 13-1/2" of beads onto the flexible wire then string the largest lampwork bead. Continue stringing beads an additional 31" then string back through the largest lampwork again. This will form a continuous loop. Complete lariat with the final 13-1/2" of wire. Attach wire to second pre-made headpin and crimp in place.

This feminine lariat is just perfect to spruce up that plain black dress! It's a romantic lariat with its focus on Adriana's lampwork beads.

How-to:
See Rosary Turns in Basic
How-to Techniques, page
138.

SUSPENSION RINGS

"I feel that these beads convey the essence of Fiesta in the simplest way possible."

Finished length: 3"

Earrings
Lampwork by Adriana Sauceda
Design by Susan Ray

Supplies Needed

- 4 Fiesta lampwork beads
- 20 gauge silver wire, 16"
- 2 sterling silver head pins, 3" length each
- 4 sterling silver beads, 4mm
- 6 black onyx beads, 6mm
- 8 black onyx beads ,2mm

TIP: String beads onto the head pins and create rosary turns. Cut away excess wire. Cut the sterling silver wire into two pieces – 8" in length each. Make a simple rosary turn at one end of each sterling silver wire attaching the pre-strung head pin loop as you go. String the lampwork and onyx beads onto the sterling wire. Complete by stringing the silver bead at top. Turn the wire over your thumb and forefinger to create the fishhook earring. Use a ready-made earring as the form. Bend wire back and cut away any excess wire. Ola!

To feature the fine quality of this handmade lampwork in a simple, fun fashion, we highlighted the beads by creating earring drops. Allowing the beads to stand alone added visual focus.

SUSPENSION RINGS

Glass can occur naturally as obsidian, which is made when volcanic lava cools so fast that it cannot crystallize, and as "lightning stones" formed when a lightning bolt fuses ash with sand.

How-to:
See Rosary Turns in Basic How-to Techniques, page 138.

CHINOISERIE

Necklace
Lampwork by Roberta Ogborn
Design by Susan Ray

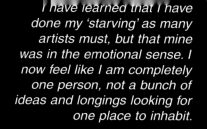

Adversity is said to be a wellspring for artistry. This saying rings true for lampworker Roberta Ogborn. As a child, "Bobbi" (as she is called by family and friends), endured the restrictions of a spinal deformity, lived in 16 foster homes, and narrowly escaped death by fire. Fortunately, the artistic outcome to her adversity is the hundreds of extraordinary beads she now makes at her Florida studio, Serendipity Suite.

Roberta's eye for lampwork started when she was just five years old. "My 'uncle' Clarence took me to the Orange Show in San Bernardino," recalls Roberta. "Perched on his shoulders, I watched a lampworker make glass animals and beads. I was totally fascinated. I remember starting to cry as we walked away, because I just wanted to stay and watch the process forever!"

Early in her life, Roberta found that art could be an escape from emotional and physical woes. She mastered sewing and painting, was a potter for several years, acquired a complete woodworking shop, was an advanced gardener and, briefly, a professional singer. Stained glass was a passion for awhile, but that medium sometimes failed to command her complete attention.

At the age of 50, an injury at work made her look for things she could do that might allow her to take care of herself and provide a needed diversion. Roberta's daughter-in-law suggested that she check out eBay's lampworking section.

"Suddenly I was five years old again, sitting on Uncle Clarence's shoulder watching the melting glass," says Roberta of that seminal moment. "All that fascination and longing came back to me so strong I could taste it!"

Two big problems remained; one was money, the other was Roberta's fear of fire.

When she was three years old, Roberta was in a foster home that caught fire. She recalls hearing the flames, feeling the heat, and seeing the fireman come to the rescue. She knew that she

Roberta I. Ogborn

ARTIST'S CONTACT INFORMATION

Roberta I. Ogborn
E-mail: roggborn@msn.com
EBay user ID: trappedinabead
Web site: roggborn1.homestead.com

A bead worth buying is anything that you just have to have. Art is so subjective that even what to me would be obvious "flaws" to someone else might just be the cat's meow. I can tell you more about what a good bead is than what a bad bead is. A good bead appeals to your physical senses (touch and sight) while a fantastic bead sings to your soul with an unforgettable melody.

—Roberta I. Ogborn

would have to overcome her fear of fire before she could even begin to learn lampworking.

"I started by buying an inexpensive kit off the Internet. It included a 'how-to' book on bead making. I memorized that book while the kit sat under the coffee table for two months. Every time I picked up the book, the longing became stronger and stronger until one day when Susan, my daughter-in-law, and I were in town, I stopped at the hardware store and bought a can of gas fuel for the torch. That night after dinner, Susan came over and we took turns on the torch. I would try a bead and she would try a bead, all the time reading and talking each other through each step of the way."

At the time, Roberta was still very much involved with stained glass, so, while her daughter-in-law used the Moretti rods that came with the kit, Roberta experimented with some of the stained glass pieces she had. She still likes to use stained glass in her beads.

"Stained glass is manufactured from the start to absorb and transmit light and nothing is as beautiful, in my opinion, as a piece of glass reflecting the spectrum of light."

Now, not so many years later, Roberta is a renowned bead artist selling her unique creations on the Internet. She reminds us that expensive equipment is not needed to make beautiful works of art that others want to buy. "I saw someone selling beads on the Internet the other day that were over 400 years old; I'll bet that bead maker didn't have a computer controlled kiln. Having the fanciest or latest model kiln does not a good bead maker make," insists Roberta.

"So here I am at 56: a lampworker! And I still get so excited about possible color combinations and techniques with manipulating the glass that I will get up in the middle of the night to work on the torch. I have so much time to make up. I have learned that I have done my 'starving' as many artists must, but my starvation was in the emotional sense. I now feel like I am completely one person, not a bunch of ideas and longings looking for one place to inhabit. My eBay username says it all really; I will forever be "trappedinabead." ☻

Rupert in the Rose Garden. This charming, if somewhat cross-eyed, garden snake is made from Moretti glass. He thinks he is in love with that sweet young thing at the other end of the garden—his own tail. He has been gathering rose buds for her! "I see life as some others are living it," says Rupert's creator Roberta Ogborn.

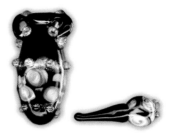

Roman **Tear Bottle.** "It's a replica of the tiny bottles Roman ladies would use to catch their tears and then present them to their men as they were going off to war," explains Roberta. "I really liked the romance behind this tradition," muses Roberta.

This **Chintz Roses** on Periwinkle bead set was inspired by a rocking chair owned by Roberta's foster grandmother. Roberta remembers it being covered in a fabric "all bright and shiny with big, cabbage-type roses on it." The glass is Moretti.

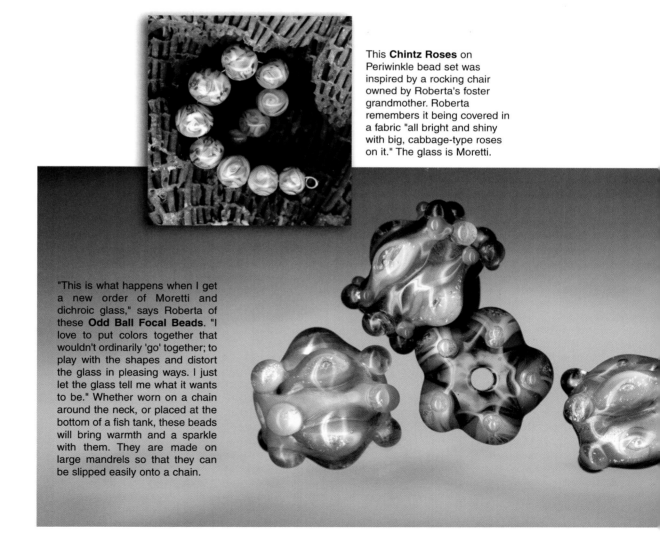

"This is what happens when I get a new order of Moretti and dichroic glass," says Roberta of these **Odd Ball Focal Beads.** "I love to put colors together that wouldn't ordinarily 'go' together; to play with the shapes and distort the glass in pleasing ways. I just let the glass tell me what it wants to be." Whether worn on a chain around the neck, or placed at the bottom of a fish tank, these beads will bring warmth and a sparkle with them. They are made on large mandrels so that they can be slipped easily onto a chain.

CHINOISERIE

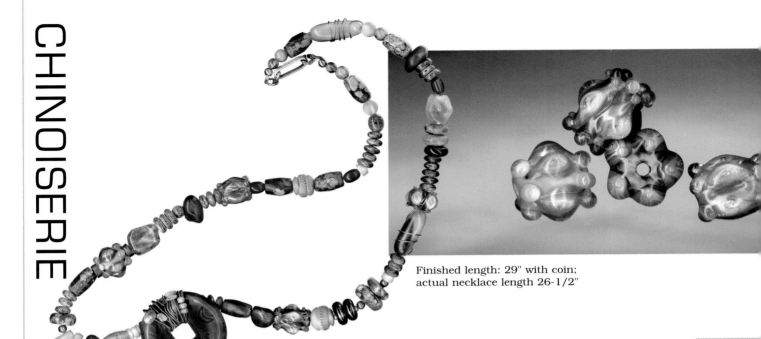

Finished length: 29" with coin;
actual necklace length 26-1/2"

This is what happens when I get a new order of Moretti and dichroic glass," says Roberta of these unusual focal beads. *"I love to put color together that wouldn't ordinarily 'go' together; to play with the shapes and distort the glass in pleasing ways.*

-Roberta Ogborn

Necklace
Lampwork by Roberta Ogborn
Design by Susan Ray

- Antique gold closure and 2 matching jump rings
- Replica Chinese coin, 45mm
- 2 crimp beads
- 32" flexible wire
- 1-1/2 yards of copper wire
- 4 Moretti glass beads
- 5 saddle brown amber or glass beads, 8mm x 6mm
- 8 turquoise barrel shaped beads, 11mm x 10 mm
- 25 square stone finished glass beads, 6mm x 6mm
- 13 heishe beads in natural and brown, 6mm
- 2 bone or ceramic horns, 25mm
- 2 bone or ceramic round beads, 15mm
- 2 natural stone barrels, 25mm x 10mm
- 2 frosted glass beads, 8mm
- 5 turquoise rondells, 11mm-12mm
- 2 transparent green druks, 6mm
- 3 turquoise round beads, 7mm
- 4 natural stone round beads, 12mm-15mm
- 6 ceramic discs, 8mm
- Ceramic oval, 10mm x 8mm
- 2 rutiled quartz beads, 18mm x 12mm
- 5 antique gold balls, 3mm x 5mm
- 7 assorted natural stone beads 2mm to 4mm (for copper wire wraps)

TIP: Wrap the copper wire through the center hole of the Chinese coin, stringing the small natural stones as you go. Lay out this large assortment of beads on your bead board. Wrap the natural stone barrels with copper wire before you begin stringing. String half of your necklace, and then string the flexible wire through the copper wire on the back of the coin. Complete by stringing the rest of the beads.

These wound beads look like they were discovered in some ancient tomb. Because of their unusual shapes and colors, each individual lampwork bead is mesmerizing. A Chinese coin and odd array of natural stone and glass beads completed the centuries-old appeal.

How-to:
See Single-strand
Necklace in Basic How-to
Techniques, page 137.

ROSE CHINTZ

My grandmother, Lula, had a rocking chair covered in a fabric all bright and shiny with big, cabbage-type roses on it." This became the inspiration for these beautiful rose beads.

-Robert Ogborn

Necklace
Lampwork by Roberta Ogborn
Design by Susan Ray

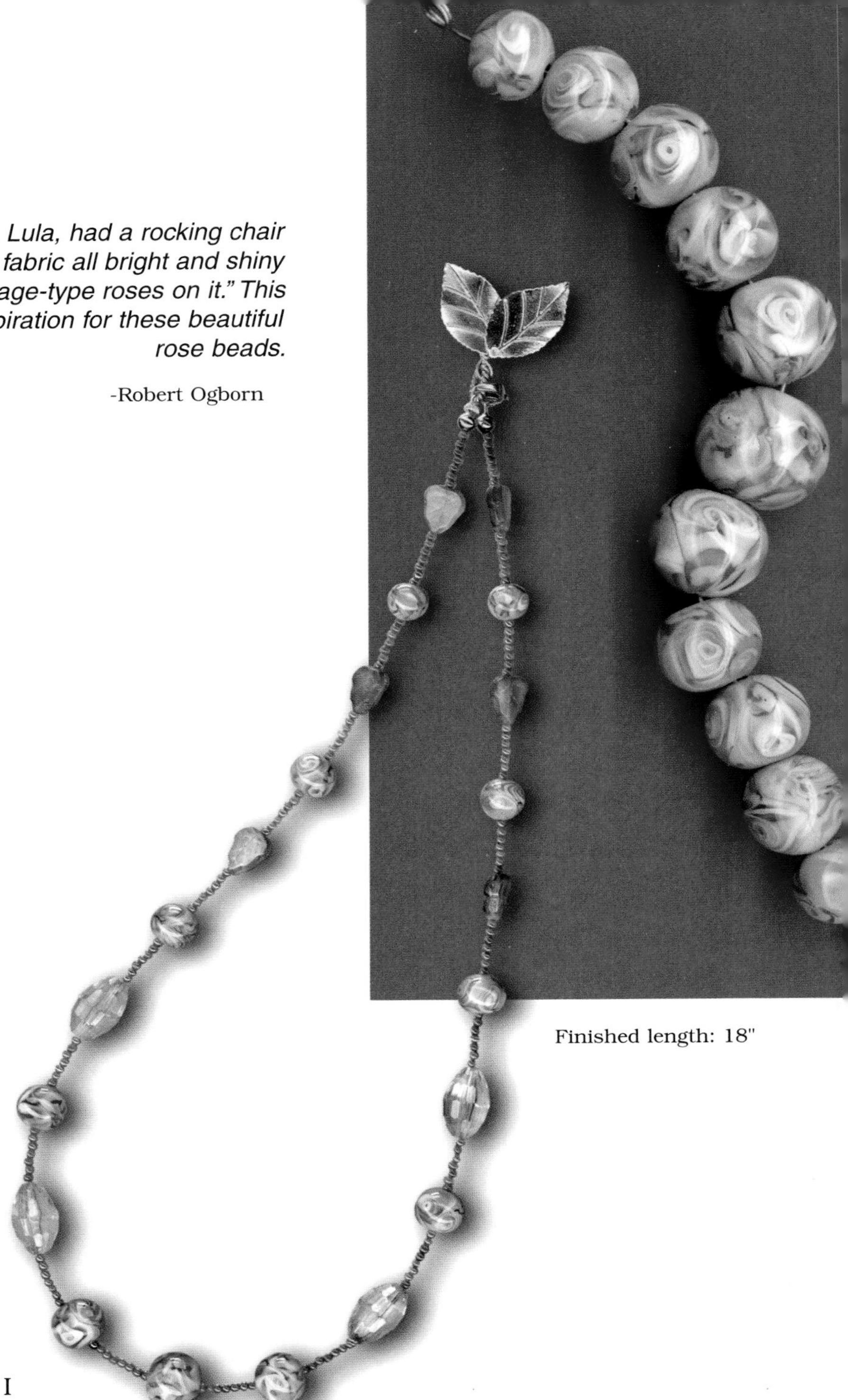

Finished length: 18"

Spring is in the air. The large cabbage roses on the squabble Moretti glass beads are so delicate that they required very little embellishment. To create a simple, unified look to the piece, I first decided on the tiny aurora borealis coated blue seed beads. Then, to add some interesting beads, the vintage faceted crystals and green pressed glass leaves were added to complete the ensemble. Although the piece is symmetrical, using three of Roberta's lampwork roses at the very center of the necklace gave them center stage.

Supplies Needed

- 2 crimp beads
- 22" flexible wire
- 11 Moretti glass rose beads graduated from 7mm-16mm
- 6 Czech pressed glass leaves, 12mm x 8mm
- 4 vintage aurora borealis faceted crystal ovals, 15mm x 10mm
- Strand of 13/0 blue aurora borealis seed beads
- 2 gold plate balls, 3.5mm (ending each length just before the crimp bead)
- 2 gold base metal leaves, 20mm x 14mm
- Gold base metal spring ring
- Gold lobster claw clasp

How-to:
See Single-strand
Necklace in Basic How-to
Techniques, page 137.

RENDEZVOUS

Necklace
Lampwork by Julie Suchy
Design by Susan Ray

I end up doing what looks good as I go along, letting the glass do what it wants as the project unfolds before me.

—Julie Suchy

Midwesterner Julie Suchy has always been artistic. She throws pottery, dabbles in calligraphy, spins wool, and has seriously pursued stained glass. But not until she discovered lampwork did she find a medium that satisfied all her needs. For her, she says, bead making requires less space and no huge time commitment. Blending technical skills with creative freedom, she believes lampwork is the essence of artistic expression. It has also proved to be the basis for an increasingly successful small business. But most of all, she says bead making is just plain fun.

"I have always loved glass," says Julie. "When I was a child, I dreamed of making stained glass windows. I grew up on a farm and broke the glass out of old cabinets in my father's workshop and saved it for the time I could make windows."

That time did come: Julie taught herself the craft of stained glass soon after she graduated from high school and for the next twenty years made full-sized leaded windows—not just small sun catchers. She says that stained glass for her has been a very rewarding, if time consuming, art form.

Her recent discovery of lampwork evolved from a chance encounter with a bead making display at the local stained glass supply store. Intrigued by what she saw there, Julie bought a book on bead making, found a free starter kit on the Internet, and started making glass beads using her husband's braising torch.

We don't know what those first beads looked like, but judging from what Julie is producing today—just three years after she picked up that book on bead making—they must have been good. Her work now is rich with imagination and color, and she is inventing new bead styles all the time. In addition to the vessel and opalescent focal pieces shown in this book, she has numerous pendants, bicones, and boro beads on her eBay site (see contact information).

"They are all sparkling little jewels to me," says Julie. She says she uses no special techniques to make her beads except perhaps to keep the annealing temperatures down to around 1050 degrees. This is for borosilicate glass, which is her favorite glass at the moment. Higher kiln temperatures can, she says, turn the glass milky.

Julie Suchy

ARTIST'S CONTACT INFORMATION

Julie Suchy
Jewels Beads
2302 W. 116 Ave.
Milan, IL 61264
E-mail: Julie@jewelsbeads.com
Web site: www.jewelsbeads.com
eBay user ID: Jewel1011

Julie's Favorite Suppliers:
Frantz Art Glass & Supply
130 W. Corporate Road
Shelton, WA 98584
(800) 839-6712
www.frantzartglass.com

Glass Alchemy, Ltd.
6539 NE 59th Place
Portland, OR 97218
(503) 460-0546
www.glassalchemyarts.com

Northstar Glassworks
9386 SW Tigard St.
Tigard, OR 97223
(866) 684-6986
www.northstarglass.com

"The changes to a bead's color that can occur in the kiln are one reason why it's nearly impossible to duplicate a bead. Many people have asked me to make a certain type of bead, but that's not easy to do because of all the variables involved. So I end up doing what looks good as I go along, letting the glass do what it wants as the project unfolds before me."

Julie insists that there is no extraordinary skill involved in bead making, just a lot of practice.

"I'm a lot better now than I was just a year ago," she says. "For example, I've discovered that the handles and the lip of a vessel take precision and careful heat control and I've learned how to do that by simple trial and error."

Julie jokes that she is "inspirationally challenged" and uses no particular resource or imagery to guide her bead making. "I just make what I like and think is beautiful and hope that other people like it too."

Julie's bead making is currently a part-time endeavor, but is starting to turn into a profession. She had to cut her full-time job as a computer drafter to part time to allow her more time in the studio. To keep up with her expanding business, she and her husband are in the process of converting part of their laundry room into a separate studio.

Her husband, a computer specialist, designed Julie's Web page, and helps with all her other computer needs. "The whole family supports my bead making," says Julie. Whether or not it becomes a full-time second career, only time will tell. But one thing is certain: bead making has taken over as the primary focus of Julie's multi-faceted artistic endeavors. "I have to say that, because of my love for beads, my stained glass tools are all packed up."

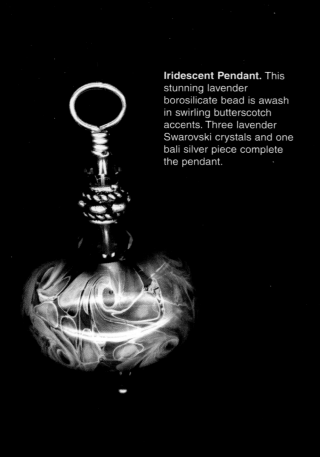

Iridescent Pendant. This stunning lavender borosilicate bead is awash in swirling butterscotch accents. Three lavender Swarovski crystals and one bali silver piece complete the pendant.

Topaz Vessel (left) and **Cobalt Vessel** (right). These Greek inspired bottles are precisely shaped, flattened, and decorated with blue and green swirls with spots of brown frit. They are made of Moretti glass.

Three single-handled **Vessels with Stoppers.** The vessel on the left is made of tan and olive Moretti glass with mauve spots that impart an organic look. The rounded bottom is typical of the ancient Greek amphora. The vessel in the center has a black Moretti base decorated with lavender frit. The rightmost vessel is also made of black Moretti glass. It is flattened and decorated with pools of brilliant blue on the body.

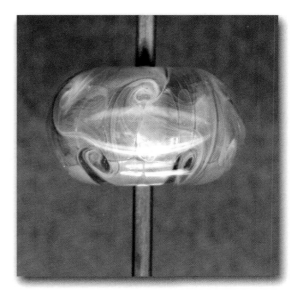

Single Borosilicate Opalescent Focal Bead. The remarkable opalescence effect of this bead is enhanced by swirling amber and purple colors.

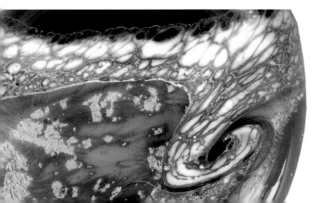

The round bottom to this single handled vessel is typical of the ancient Greek amphora.

—Julie Suchy

Necklace
Lampwork by Julie Suchy
Design by Susan Ray

Finished length: 20"

The tan-and-olive background to this Moretti glass vessel was a great neutral for a mix of mauves, lavenders, and pinks. The vessel itself became an instant highlight by stringing it to the necklace from a head pin filled with a fine cut crystal and pearl. A spring ring is strung through the vessel handle and a tiny gold heart then through a second loop made with a rosary turn. Although the piece looks simple, many varieties of beads were used to create a detailed look. Graduating the scale of the beads as they move toward the neckline add to the drama of the tiny vessel pendant.

Supplies Needed

- 6mm spring ring
- Small base metal heart with jump ring
- 2 crimp beads
- Head pin
- 24" flexible wire
- Moretti glass vessel
- 2 rhinestone roundels, 6mm
- 4 gold bell caps, 8mm
- 2 vintage faceted amethyst crystal round beads, 9mm
- Assorted pearls, crows, crystals, 4mm to 8mm
- Strand of multi-colored 6/0 beads in copper/bronze opaque patina
- Strand of transparent aurora borealis topaz 6/0 beads
- 6 gold barrel shaped spacers, 4mm
- Gold magnetic clasp
- 2 gold plate balls (ending each length just before the crimp bead), 4mm

How-to: See Single-strand
Necklace in Basic How-to
Techniques, page 137; See
Rosary Turns in Basic How-
To Techniques, page 138.

VERMEIL HARMONY

Finished Length: 26"

Necklace
Lampwork by Julie Suchy
Design by Brittany Berndston

If there ever was a genie in a bottle it is Brittany. Her charm and smile are equal to her talent at beading. One of my three wishes was to create a necklace filled with mystery and intrigue. Julie's vessels conjure up such moods. The addition of the lovely vintage vermeil came to us through a Chicago auction. Wrapped in waxed paper, we delighted in each and every piece as we unfurled the treasures. Brittany cast her eye on creating a far-away vision of vessels, mixed beads and many dangles.

Supplies Needed

- Lampwork vessel
- 170 assorted 2mm to 8mm beads
- 12 vermeil spacers
- 8 vermeil coil beads
- 2 vintage vermeil urns
- 4 gold bell caps
- 8 topaz faceted discs, 8mm to 10mm
- 16 gold headpins
- 30" flexible wire
- 2 brass crimp beads
- Vermeil "s" clasp
- 4 vermeil round balls, 3mm

How-to: See Single Strand
Necklace in Basic How-to
Techniques, page 137; See
Rosary Turn in Basic How-to
Techniques, page 138.

TABBIES & GARNETS

Ensemble
Lampwork by Rhonda Harris
Design by Trent Meisner

Rhonda Harris grew up in Saugus, Massachusetts and, in 1989, moved to Santa Cruz on the central California coast where, along with her cat "Spanky," she has been exploring her artistic side.

Santa Cruz, of course, is the perfect place to stretch one's creative limbs. It's a large artist community filled with shops and galleries, settled along a cozy bay and adjoined by dense pine forests where one can get pleasantly lost.

"Ever since I've moved here my artistic energy has been going full speed," says Rhonda enthusiastically about her surroundings.

She began right away working with glass, painting on whole panes and selling her work in local stores and galleries. "I've always wanted to work with glass, and painting on it seemed a natural thing to do," says Rhonda.

However, she soon discovered lampworking. "I went to a bead store to look for some pieces of glass to incorporate into my art," she explains. "There, the owner was demonstrating beads. After watching for five minutes, I tried my hand at it and was just amazed at the results. In contrast to a painting, which can take months to complete, beads were instant!"

Rhonda says that for years, she had dreamt about becoming a glassblower, but the thought of renting space and equipment dissuaded her. "My dreams were answered when I found a smaller version of it, something I could do in my own living room. I bought the glass kit, a small torch and gas tank, and have been seriously addicted to bead making ever since."

"Lampworking gives me the opportunity to create objects using glistening, colorful surfaces and a wide range of forms," says Rhonda. "Creating with glass offers endless possibilities; I find that I am forever trying to express the shapes, colors, and techniques that are inside me."

Constantly at Rhonda's side is Spanky, her "handsome and sweet" cat—ah, we mean assistant.

"Spanky is just as much a part of these beads as I am," Rhonda insists. "He sits by me throughout the entire process. Maybe he just likes the hissing of the flame, but I like to think he is helping to direct the creative process. Whichever it is, the fact that he tirelessly

Rhonda Harris

ARTIST'S CONTACT INFORMATION

Rhonda Harris
Spanky's Lampwork Studio
PO Box 1805
Aptos, CA 95001
(831) 464-1703
E-mail: harrisrhonda@sbcglobal.net
eBay user ID: spankyslampworkbeads

> *I look forward to years and years of creating glass subjects. I'm soon going to incorporate my small glass sculptures into my larger glass paintings. This will open up a whole new path for me. I'm also looking forward to designing high-end quality jewelry. I'm combining my newest craft "Precious Metal Clay" with my glass and I cannot wait to see the results. I envision amazing art pieces.*
>
> —Rhonda Harris

sits by me gives me the creative boost I need. Believe it or not, I will sit there thinking what to do next, and all I have to do is look at him and an idea just pops into my head."

"We especially like trying to come up with techniques that are unique. We work with mostly borosilicate glass which is a little stiffer and harder to work with than other types of glass, but the range of designs this glass offers is virtually infinite, which makes the extra effort worth it."

Rhonda admits that the borosilicates can be somewhat darker than other types of glass, and only fully appreciated out of doors in the sunlight. Consequently, she strives to make her creations look great indoors so that they are absolutely stunning outside.

She is also experimenting with new techniques. "I'm teaching myself to do larger, more sculpted glass pieces that rest on hollow tubing and have no mandrels. With most of my art, I just dive in. I have never had the patience for sitting and being instructed, so I am basically self-taught."

Through practice, Rhonda now excels at using "stringers"—threads of molten glass applied to the surface of the bead. "Working with stringers takes some getting used to," says Rhonda. "But once you do it, it can take you to different realms. The patterns and designs are endless. I especially love dark patterns against a light background. They provide for lots of movement and room for dreaming."

Over the past three years, Rhonda says so many other lampwork artists have inspired her. But now she largely finds her inspiration in beautiful photographs of landscapes or animals. Rhonda's favorite theme for beads are animal prints, especially of the feline variety. "I love the abstract, so you will rarely see me doing your basic dots-on-dots. I cannot just make a certain style or design on demand," says Rhonda. "It almost always comes off the top of my head."

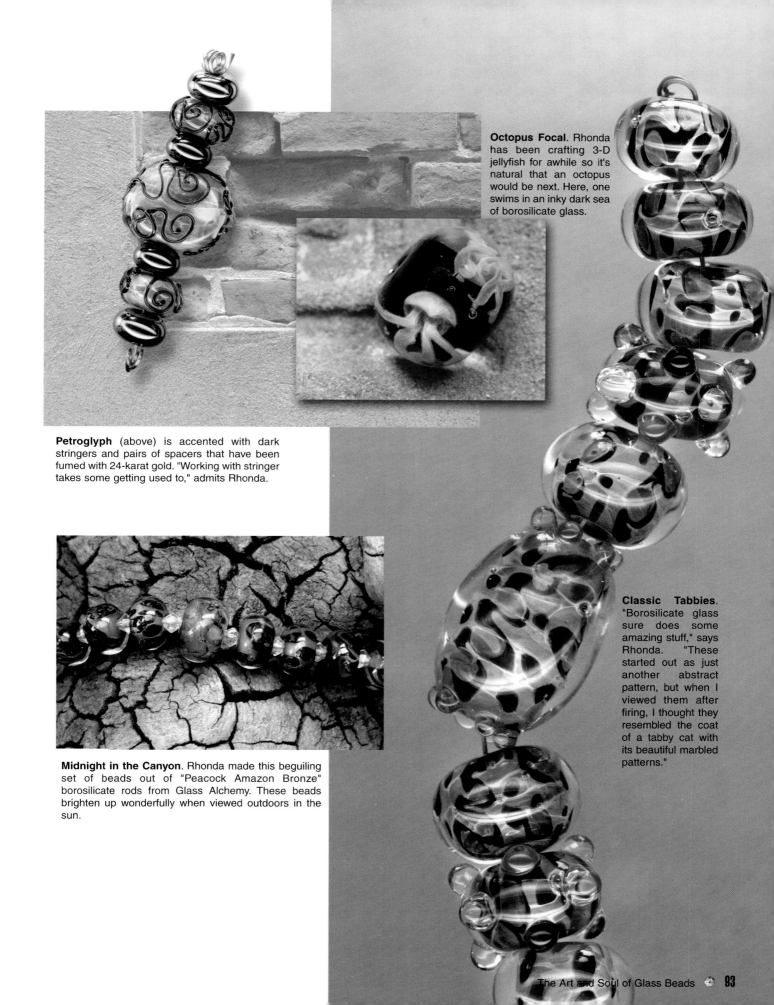

Octopus Focal. Rhonda has been crafting 3-D jellyfish for awhile so it's natural that an octopus would be next. Here, one swims in an inky dark sea of borosilicate glass.

Petroglyph (above) is accented with dark stringers and pairs of spacers that have been fumed with 24-karat gold. "Working with stringer takes some getting used to," admits Rhonda.

Classic Tabbies. "Borosilicate glass sure does some amazing stuff," says Rhonda. "These started out as just another abstract pattern, but when I viewed them after firing, I thought they resembled the coat of a tabby cat with its beautiful marbled patterns."

Midnight in the Canyon. Rhonda made this beguiling set of beads out of "Peacock Amazon Bronze" borosilicate rods from Glass Alchemy. These beads brighten up wonderfully when viewed outdoors in the sun.

TABBIES & GARNETS

Three Piece Ensemble
Lampwork by Rhonda Harris
Design by Trent Meisner

Trent has balanced the beautifully marbled pattern in these sparkling borosilicate "tabbie" glass beads with garnets and hematite. Trent's talent is an inspiration. His use of garnets and hematite enlightens the ensemble that is equally fit for evening attire or sleek enough for a daytime business suit.

Necklace
Finished Length: 17"

- 1" borosilicate glass focal bead
- 34 hand cut garnet rectangles, 6x4mm
- 30 hematite tubes, 2mm x 6mm
- 2 round hematite beads, 2mm
- 2 hematite barrels, 6mm x 4mm
- 2 hematite discs 3mm to 4mm
- 2 crimp beads
- 21" flexible wire
- Lobster claw and spring ring

Bracelet
Finished Length: 7-1/2"

Note: Although the finished size of this bracelet is 7-1/2", the depth of the lampwork may require you to add some length for proper fit.

- 8 hand cut garnet rectangles, 6mm x 4mm
- 6 hematite rectangles 6mm x 4mm
- 4 hematite discs 3mm to 4mm
- 2 hematite tubes 2mm x 6mm
- 2 hematite round beads 2mm
- 2 crimp beads
- 12" flexible wire
- Lobster claw and spring ring

Earrings
Finished Length: 1-1/2"

- 2 sterling silver 3" headpins
- 2 sterling silver earwires with ball and coil
- 2 hematite tubes 2mm x 4mm
- 4 hand cut garnet tubes 2mm x 3mm
- 2 hematite discs, 2mm

Supplies Needed

Supplies Needed

Supplies Needed

TABBIES & GARNETS

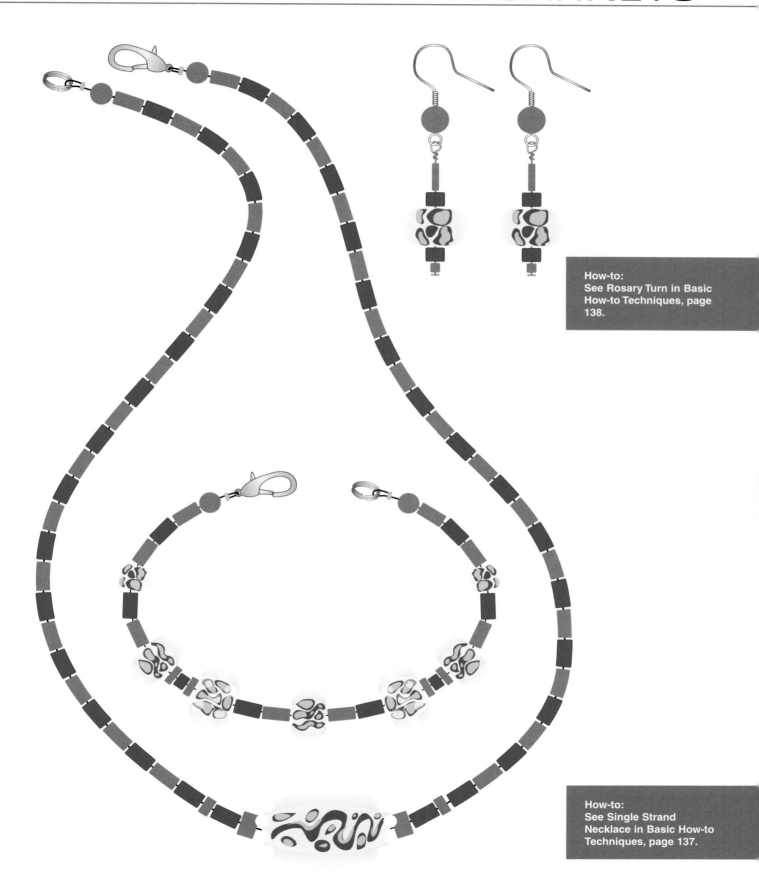

How-to:
See Rosary Turn in Basic How-to Techniques, page 138.

How-to:
See Single Strand Necklace in Basic How-to Techniques, page 137.

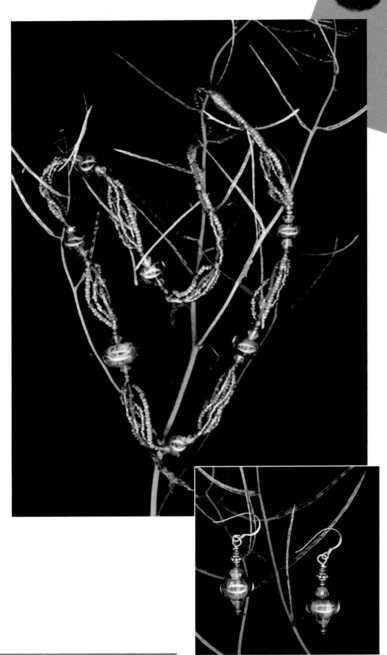

- 3-7 lampwork beads (always an odd number is a general rule to make necklace hang well)
- Twice as many crystal or metal beads to bracket the lampwork beads. This will call attention to the lampwork beads. Select a color from the lampwork bead OR go with gold, silver or copper. When I refer to "feature beads", I mean the lampwork beads and these bracketing beads. The overall effect is of several strands of seed beads between lampworked beads. The Lampwork beads are 'bracketed' by crystals or metallics which are chosen specifically to bring out the more subtle colors the artist has included in the lampworked beads.
- Bobbin of "D" nymo or the finest silamide thread
- Smallest needle you can get the thread through!
- Seed beads in a variety of colors selected from the lampwork beads.

p.s. One thing that cannot be taught or instructed is color. Remember that you want people to look at the lampworked beads and see the subtle colors. This is why I say to choose a crystal or metallic bead to bracket the lampwork, and recommend that you pick up a color that is subtle in the lampwork beads. This will draw attention to the beads and make people look deeply into the bead to see that bit of sparkle or small touch of a contrasting color they might otherwise miss. The seed beads are not as important as the beads you use to bracket the lampwork beads and their colors can be any colors and textures taken from the larger beads.

MIDNIGHT BLUES

1. First step is to determine the overall length of necklace and distance between lampwork beads. This is most easily done using a measured bead board, but you can also use a measuring tape or even string. Thread needle with a double length of "D" nymo thread at least twice desired length of necklace. String the necklace, using seed beads to space the lampwork beads at desired location. Once you have a one-strand necklace, use a mirror and hold the necklace up to ensure that you can see all of the lampwork beads, have the correct length for your neckline and hairstyle and personal taste. Make adjustments at this point. The necklace will not lie correctly yet, as the one length of seed beads and thread is NOT strong enough to support the weight of the lampwork beads.

2. At the last two inches of the necklace, the part that will be behind your neck, count out seven seed beads, then a different color (or even a larger seed bead), then back to seven seed beads, stringing the different color/size every seven beads, ending with a loop of fifteen beads, and back through the second color bead. Now you'll be turning around and heading back towards the front of the necklace. Again seven beads, and through the second color single bead. This will form a series of loops that will allow you to adjust the length of the necklace using an "S" hook.

3. When you reach the part of the necklace that will be at your shoulder (i.e., the part of the necklace that will show in front), chose a second color of seed beads from the art bead, and string a second strand between the featured beads. When you get to the back of the necklace, you'll be reinforcing the loops you'll be using for the clasp. These beads will have a lot of thread going through them, which is why you need the finest needle possible.

4. Repeat the process until you have at least three strands of seed beads between the featured beads. From there on, it will be a matter of judgment and taste. The heavier the lampwork beads, the more strands of seed beads you'll need to make the necklace lay well (otherwise your largest center bead will pull the entire necklace down into a "V" rather than a "U"). In this case there are seven strands of seed beads supporting the sets of feature beads.

5. When you get short on thread, make sure you leave enough to tie a knot and start over. Try to arrange it so that your knots are near the larger beads; it'll be easier to work around them that way. I wait until I'm through with the entire necklace, then thread ends through a dozen or so beads, and snip excess. "Big Eye' needles are not fine enough for most of the work, but are great for tucking in the odds and ends of threads where you have to knot them.

How-to:
See Multi-Strand
Bracelets
in Basic How-to
Techniques, page 137.

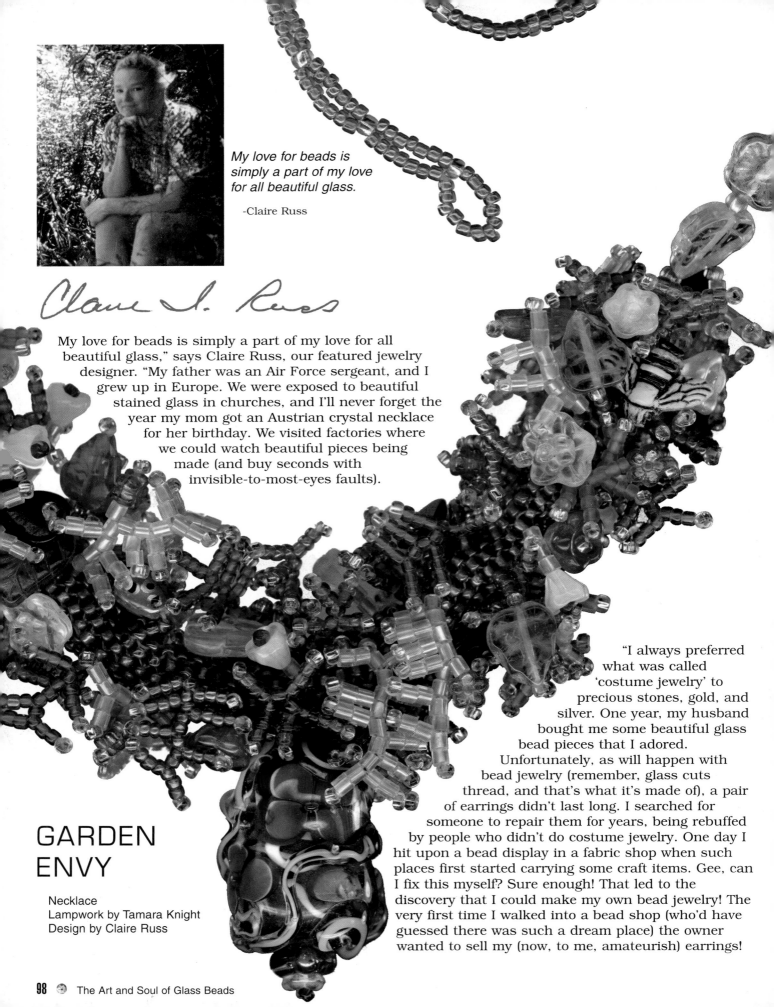

*My love for beads is
simply a part of my love
for all beautiful glass.*

-Claire Russ

Claire J. Russ

My love for beads is simply a part of my love for all
beautiful glass," says Claire Russ, our featured jewelry
designer. "My father was an Air Force sergeant, and I
grew up in Europe. We were exposed to beautiful
stained glass in churches, and I'll never forget the
year my mom got an Austrian crystal necklace
for her birthday. We visited factories where
we could watch beautiful pieces being
made (and buy seconds with
invisible-to-most-eyes faults).

GARDEN ENVY

Necklace
Lampwork by Tamara Knight
Design by Claire Russ

"I always preferred
what was called
'costume jewelry' to
precious stones, gold, and
silver. One year, my husband
bought me some beautiful glass
bead pieces that I adored.
Unfortunately, as will happen with
bead jewelry (remember, glass cuts
thread, and that's what it's made of), a pair
of earrings didn't last long. I searched for
someone to repair them for years, being rebuffed
by people who didn't do costume jewelry. One day I
hit upon a bead display in a fabric shop when such
places first started carrying some craft items. Gee, can
I fix this myself? Sure enough! That led to the
discovery that I could make my own bead jewelry! The
very first time I walked into a bead shop (who'd have
guessed there was such a dream place) the owner
wanted to sell my (now, to me, amateurish) earrings!

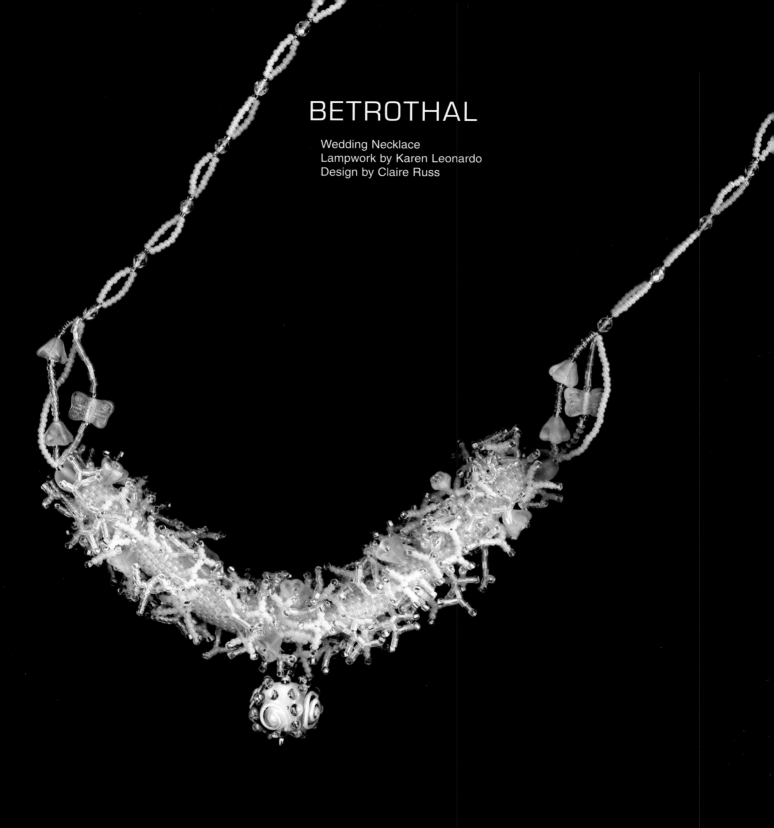

BETROTHAL

Wedding Necklace
Lampwork by Karen Leonardo
Design by Claire Russ

After my husband retired, we did like good retirees and moved to Florida. That lasted six years–we just didn't have it in us to be good Florida retirees. So we sold most of what we owned, bought an RV, and hit the road for three years. I bought a large Rubbermaid chest for my beading supplies, kept my magazine subscriptions up, and looked for bead shops everywhere. Soon after we resettled in our new home in Galena, Illinois, with Susan Ray's bead shop within walking distance! It's as close to a happy ending as I can think of for this story (although no end is in sight!)."

Claire's Jewelry can be seen at Bubbles, Bangles, and Beads, 234 N. Main St., Galena, IL 61036.

LUNA MOTH
FANTASY

Necklace
Lampwork by David Jurgens
Design by Susan Ray

I never thought such deep expressions of myself could be captured on such a small surface such as a bead.

—David Jurgens

Like many bead artists, David Jurgens is primarily self-taught. But in his case, this fact is not a matter of economic necessity or limited resources. The fact is, David purposely has never taken a class in bead making, preferring instead to develop his own distinctive technique and style.

From the moment he uncrated his first torch and box of glass, David has followed only books and other references. This sink-or-swim approach has paid off in a spectacular way. Along with the creations of our other Hawaiian resident, David's wife Rebecca, his rather large, intricate beads have a devoted group of buyers on the Internet and in retail stores throughout the mainland. But such was not always the case.

David Jurgens was born in San Diego, California. Having been drawn to the piano from early childhood, he considered music his primary artistic outlet. Then, as he tells the story, his passion for glass "was ignited" in the summer of 1997 while strolling through Seattle with his wife Rebecca. There, they saw a glassblower working his craft for an audience. "I mentioned to my wife how neat it would be to learn that art but I never knew how much she heard those words," says David.

At the time, David was busy meeting the numerous commitments of being on active duty in the Navy. "My refuge in music had been fading for some time and it was time for a new outlet," recalls David. "My wife Becky went out of her way to set me up with the equipment I needed."

David found the assortment of glass rods and the torch somewhat daunting at first, but felt instant exhilaration being able to create something with his own hands from what he called a "rainbow of colors." And he continued to do it on his own, proving that anyone with an artistic flair can pick up the craft of bead making in his or her spare time.

ARTIST'S CONTACT INFORMATION

David Jurgens
L and S Arts
94-155 Hokuala Place
Mililani, HI 96789
(808) 623-3102
E-mail: landsart1@aol.com
Web site: www.landsart.com
eBay user ID: landsart

Favorite Bead Shop:
Fusion Beads
1111 NW Leary Way
Ballard, WA 98107
206 782 4595

Our major sales come from the eBay auction house. We have been full time with them since 1997. Most of our customers are designers wanting custom pieces and we have quite a few collectors too.

We could have avoided several mistakes and setbacks in our work by going to a few classes; however, it may have compromised the refinement of the individual styles we have nurtured.

—David Jurgens

"Sure, I could have signed up for a class or two to learn someone else's technique. But this was something I wanted to forge through on my own."

David says he made many mistakes at first and, in hindsight, was lucky he never blew himself up! But in the end he had a style that was all his own.

For his inspiration, David says he draws on natural surroundings, his own fantasies, and on God. Each piece showcases a particular theme with evocative names like "Emerald Koi Pond," "Blue Lagoon," or "Polar Islands." As a piece is being created, David insists that "it takes on its own form and features that could never have been planned ahead."

Every bead he makes is also a window to his soul, says David. "Sometimes I feel as if I am just a vessel for a divine idea, the design to come through my hands. It sounds rather corny—but it's true. I never thought such deep expressions of myself could be captured on such a small surface such as a bead."

Others agree, judging from the success David has had sharing his unique creations on a Web site he operates with his wife, Becky, and on eBay where he has been selling under the user name Landsart since 1997. David also teaches at bead shows and private studios.

"If someone would have told me 10 years ago this is what I would be doing in retirement I would have labeled them 'crazy.' I think it's those 'crazy' notions in life that keeps us all sane—if that makes sense."

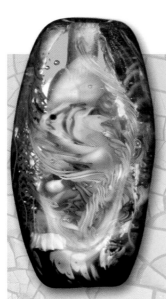

This **Aquarium** bead with its delicate sulfa theme uses several different types of complex latticino within its three encased layers. The use of dichroic glass, metals, and frit add depth and reality. The bead is made of Moretti glass.

Iridescent blue dichroic glass brilliantly accents this **Burgundy on Cream** Moretti glass focal bead. David Jurgens draws on his imagination and fantasy for inspiration.

These delicious encased **Floral Garden** beads are inspired by David's "feminine side."

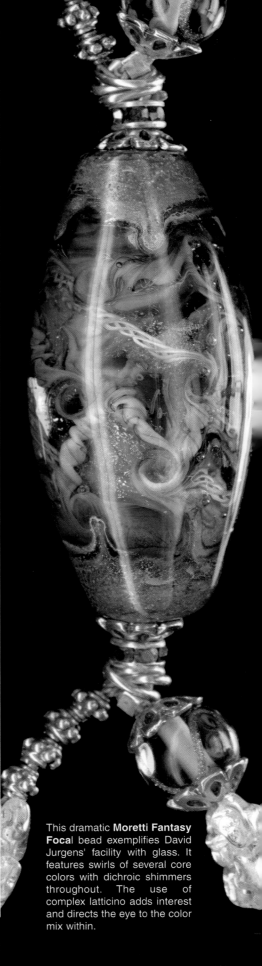

This dramatic **Moretti Fantasy Focal** bead exemplifies David Jurgens' facility with glass. It features swirls of several core colors with dichroic shimmers throughout. The use of complex latticino adds interest and directs the eye to the color mix within.

LUNA MOTH FANTASY

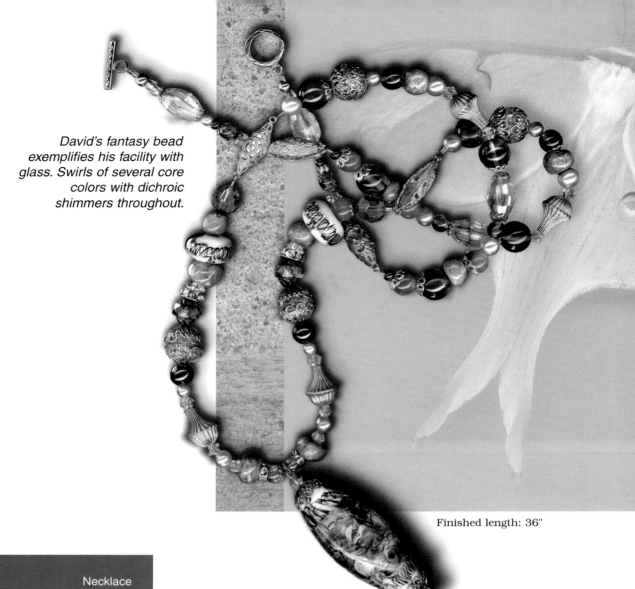

David's fantasy bead exemplifies his facility with glass. Swirls of several core colors with dichroic shimmers throughout.

Finished length: 36"

Necklace
Lampwork by David Jurgens
Design by Susan Ray

The special, shimmering quality of David's bead appealed to the romantic bell caps and vintage faceted barrel crystals. This necklace is fit for a princess!

Supplies Needed

- Gold plate toggle clasp
- 2 crimp beads
- 40" flexible wire
- Lampwork bead, 55mm
- 2 lampwork side beads, 16mm
- 2 gold crimp beads
- Gold head pin, 4"
- 4 rhinestone rondells, 8mm
- 14 pearls, 4mm to 8mm
- 15 bicones, 5mm x 10mm
- 9 gold lined seed beads, 6/0
- 8 ceramic blue beads, 9mm
- Assorted faceted crystals, round vitrails, amethyst druks, vintage barrel, and round crystals 12mm and 15mm x 10mm
- 4 dozen bell caps, varying sizes
- 2 vintage bell shaped beads
- 2 topaz cathedrals
- 2 gold plate balls (ending each length just before the crimp bead), 4mm

TIP: Make the pendant first then string to the necklace at the center.

How-to: See Single-strand Necklace in Basic How-to Techniques, page 137; See Rosary Turn in Basic How-to Techniques, page 138.

HAWAIIAN WATERS

The delicate sulfa theme uses several different types of complex latticino within its three encased layers.

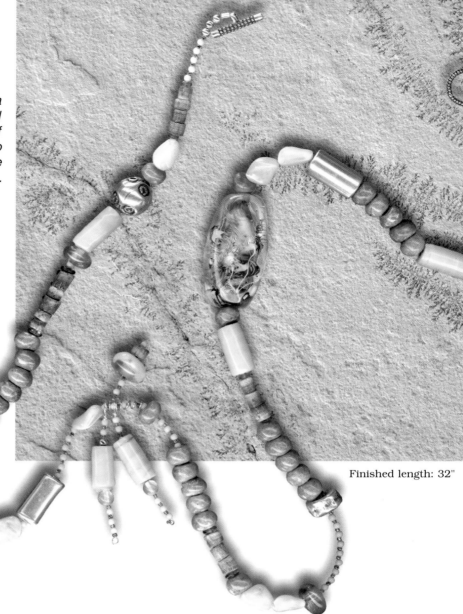

Finished length: 32"

Necklace
Lampwork by David Jurgens
Design by Susan Ray

David is a master at complex beads. The mastery of the focal lampwork bead, and its grand size, require the use of simple forms and shapes to offset it. If you look closely, you can actually see air bubbles from the fish. I just want to feed them!

Supplies Needed

- Toggle clasp
- 2 crimp beads
- 38" flexible wire
- Moretti glass bead, 42mm
- 6 silver beads, 3mm to 4mm
- 5 hollow silver beads, 5mm x 12mm to 20mm x 10mm
- 25 ceramic beads, 10mm
- 6 ceramic barrels, 20mm x 10mm
- 9 mother of pearl beads, 14mm x 5mm
- 3 transparent rose side beads
- Opaque rose/white side bead
- 7" sterling silver wire for coiling
- Assorted seed beads, 11/0, 13/0, 6/0
- 3 eye pins, 3" in length
- Spring ring
- 2 sterling silver balls (ending each length just before the crimp bead)

TIP: Make the tassel ends first; set it aside until the necklace is complete. Attach the tassels to a spring ring and then attach the spring ring to the necklace.

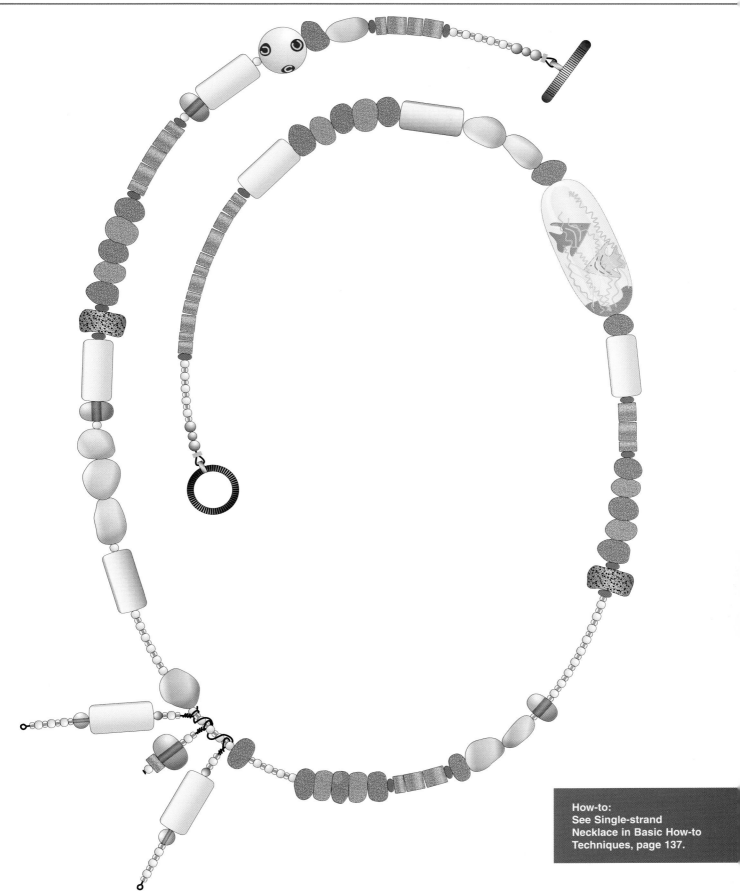

How-to:
See Single-strand
Necklace in Basic How-to
Techniques, page 137.

UNICORN
MYTH

Necklace and Earrings
Lampwork by Rebecca Jurgens
Design by Susan Ray

*I have always felt beads are
tiny facets of myself.*

—Rebecca Jurgens

Art has always been a source of endless possibility for
Rebecca Jurgens. As a teenager, Rebecca took formal classes in
oil painting, later adding watercolor, acrylics, and air brushing to
her palette. When times were tough financially, she simply
switched to her mother's eyeliner and eye shadow. It was her late
father, Rebecca says, who urged her to continue with her art
during those difficult times, and to whom she owes much of her
present success. Ironically though, it wasn't until her "non-
artistic" husband (see David Jurgens) urged her to give bead
making a try, that glass came into her life.

Rebecca tells of the fateful day when she and her husband
came home after visiting Pioneer Square in Seattle, and he
mentioned how much fun it would be to learn glasswork of the
sort they saw being demonstrated that day. A seed had been
sown, and at the next opportunity Becky found herself ordering
a lampworking starter kit not for her, but for husband Dave.
Several months passed before the torch was finally fired up in
their garage, but after that, says Rebecca, there was no turning
back for Dave; "He was hooked."

It took some prodding from Dave to get Becky to try the
medium. "I was a bit paranoid when we first started out; I viewed
this entire enterprise more as a fire hazard than anything else,"
she confesses. But as soon as she saw the offspring of her efforts
emerge from the kiln the next morning, she immediately fell in
love with what she calls the "depth and expression of the
medium."

With Rebecca's conversion came the "torch wars." According to
Dave, Becky won out on bench time. But, in the end, they both
embraced their new medium with equal enthusiasm and with
comparable success. Dave now acknowledges that glass working
was the vehicle that enabled him to share his wife's long-time
love of art.

After six years of lampworking, Rebecca insists it is "still like
Christmas morning" when she opens up the kiln. Since glass
colors generally shift and change from the heated state to room
temperature, she says it is "always a surprise when you see it
cooled for the first time."

ARTIST'S CONTACT INFORMATION

Rebecca Jurgens
L and S Arts
94-155 Hokuala Place
Mililani, HI 96789
(808) 623-3102
E-mail: landsart1@aol.com
Web site: www.landsart.com
eBay user ID: landsart

Favorite Bead Books:
How to Make Lampwork Beads
by Cindy Jenkins
Contemporary Lampworking
by Bandhu Scott Dunham

Rebecca regards lampworking as a way
"to travel mentally to a whole other world,
devoid of all boundaries."

Becky and Dave made the joint decision not to seek formal instruction in bead making, preferring instead to let their own styles and techniques emerge from trial and error. They did, however, rely on books such as Cindy Jenkins' *Making Glass Beads* and Bandhu Scott Dunham's *Contemporary Lampworking*, both of which they found to be "very influential," and "valuable references still to this day."

After about a year of experimenting and refining their respective styles, they started a Web site (www.landsart.com) and, along with auctions on the Internet, things really took off.

"I think lampwork was just beginning to really catch on for the Internet when we began," Becky says. "The biggest struggle for lampworkers today is to establish and maintain a style that truly stands out from the rest. I think being self-taught has really helped us keep that window to our inner creativity open."

Rebecca's inspiration comes from many sources: Everything from ideas given her by family and customers, to the hummingbird that lands on the aloe vera plant outside their Hawaiian studio. Rebecca's mother sketches and paints beautiful horse creations, which has undoubtedly been an additional influence on her designs. Rebecca's pieces emphasize fairies, unicorns, and "anything mystical and magical." But tiny animals also capture her imagination. Lizards and geckos, which co-habitate with the Jurgens in their garage-based studio, have proved to be the perfect subjects. "They curl up on the wall behind the kiln, sticky toes keeping them in place," says Rebecca. "Then they fall asleep and allow us time to study the curves of their bodies and the overall beauty of their peaceful appearance."

It is easy to see why Rebecca regards lampworking as a way "to travel mentally to a whole other world, void of all boundaries." It's equally certain that she will not be needing to dip into the eye shadow anytime soon for want of suitable artistic media. ☻

Fantasy Gardens. This exquisite example of Rebecca Jurgen's flowing style is made of Moretti glass with custom accents. It was inspired in equal measure by Becky's love of horses and the mystical unicorn.

Sea Turtle Dreams. This sea turtle focal bead made with Moretti glass with custom style accents. The bead was inspired by the turtles Rebecca sees near her home in Hawaii. "The way they would come to the surface along the shore line to greet you was both amazing and moving."

Fairy Tales. A charming example of Rebecca Jurgens' singular craftsmanship and boundless imagination, this elf focal bead is itself a living fairy tale. Made of Moretti glass with custom style accents.

UNICORN MYTH

This bead was inspired by my equal measure of love of horses and the mystical unicorn.

—Rebecca Jurgens

Finished length: 42"

Necklace and Earrings
Lampwork by Rebecca Jurgens
Design by Susan Ray

Supplies Needed

- 36" twisted cable necklace with lobster claw clasp
- Heavy weight, sterling silver head pin
- Sterling silver bail
- 2 glass beads in amethyst, 8/0
- Glass button, 8mm x 6mm
- Silver button, 6mm x 4mm
- Spring ring

TIP: Remove the ring end of the lobster claw closure and slip the bail onto the chain. Re-attach the ring. Using the head pin and beads, create the pendant using a turn the rosary turn method. Attach the spring ring to the bail. Attach the pendant to the spring ring. Use the side beads to make a wonderful pair of matching earrings!

A warm, wool sweater and a mystical book to read, and my unicorn necklace by my side are romantic notions of an autumn day. The unicorn bead was so captivating it needed only a simple silver chain and bail to present it.

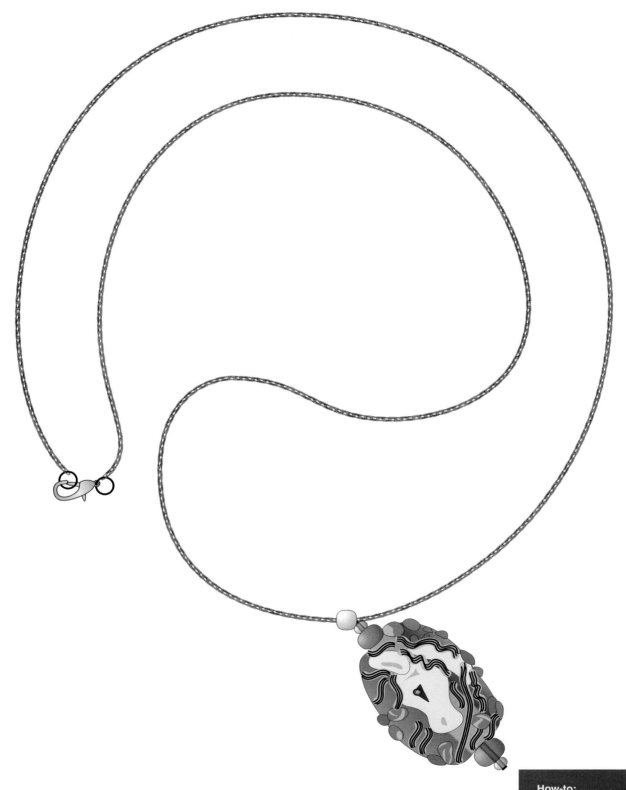

How-to:
See Rosary Turns in Basic
How-to Techniques, page
138.

SEA TURTLE

The focal bead was inspired by the turtles Rebecca sees near her home in Hawaii. "The way they come to the surface along the shoreline to greet you is both amazing and moving."

TIP: *String the two side beads close to the pendant. In this case, we strung the side beads only one inch from the pendant. This helps to properly weight the pendant on the necklace.*

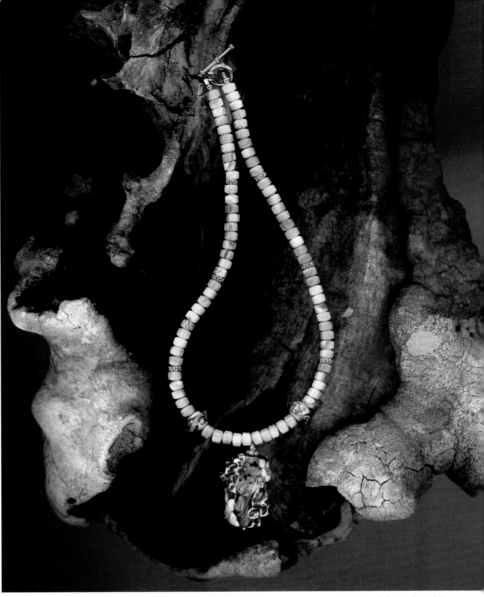

Finished length: 19"

Necklace
Lampwork by Rebecca Jurgens
Design by Susan Ray

The heft of this fine art glass bead required

necklace weight. The natural stone buttons

were just right. The natural stone also seems

so compatible with Rebecca's sea turtle bead.

The fit was perfect. We hope you agree.

- Turtle lampwork bead, 40mm in length
- 2 side beads, 12mm
- Heavy gauge half-hard sterling silver head pin, 4" in length
- Strand of natural stone buttons, 8mm x 4mm
- Heavy gauge spring ring
- 2 crimp beads
- 23" flexible wire
- Sterling silver toggle clasp
- 7 sterling silver spacers
- 4 sterling silver balls (one each ending each length just before the crimp bead and one each ending each side of pendant lampwork ensemble.)

TIP: *String the large pendant bead and silver beads and spacer on the head pin and make the rosary turn. Set aside. String the pendant at the center of the necklace using the loop from the rosary turn or add a spring ring and attach the pendant from the spring ring. The spring ring will allow you to remove the pendant and use it elsewhere as desired.*

How-to: See Single-strand Necklace in Basic How-to Techniques, page 137; See Rosary Turns in Basic How-to Techniques, page 138.

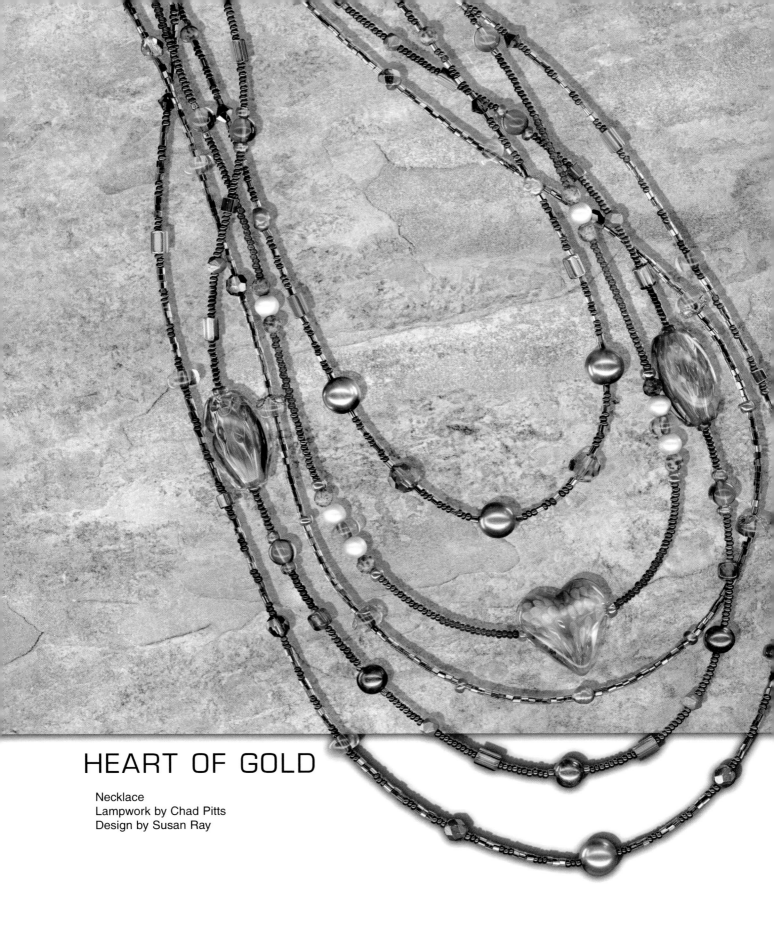

HEART OF GOLD

Necklace
Lampwork by Chad Pitts
Design by Susan Ray

With stints as a successful painter, potter, and professional glassblower under his belt, Chad Pitts had already accumulated a large dollop of artistic experience by the time he discovered the rewards of bead making. Although he still enjoys painting, it's the latter medium that has afforded him more artistic leeway and, with his beads appearing in magazines and galleries across the country, more recognition than any of his earlier endeavors.

Chad grew up in the small town of Hubbard, Ohio, near Youngstown. He sold his first painting at the age of 16 (it was a watercolor of a puppy). After high school, he attended an art school in Pittsburgh, ostensibly to launch a career in graphic design. However, that was not to be.

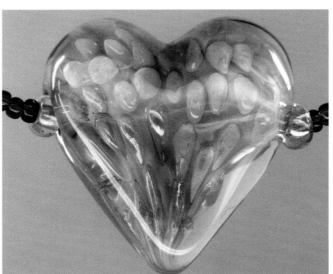

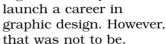

"It took about a year for me to realize that I didn't want to pursue a career in the graphic art field because of the stressful nature of the business," relates Chad. "Also, as a stubborn artist, I didn't like people directing my art."

Chad eventually moved to Virginia Beach, Virginia, where he earned a living constructing houses and found time to paint. His paintings have been featured in regional magazines and numerous galleries. Then, in 1997, he learned that a local company was accepting apprentices to make glass figurines.

"After watching someone manipulate molten glass into a beautiful figurine, I could think of nothing but the endless opportunities this medium had to offer," says Chad. "I was hooked!"

ARTIST'S CONTACT INFORMATION

Chad Pitts
Art Attacks & Strokes
Virginia Beach, VA
(757) 463-4203
E-mail: info@artattacksandstrokes.com
Web site: www.artattacksandstrokes.com
eBay user ID:
boro-guy

Chad Pitts' Favorite Suppliers
Wale Apparatus
PO Box D
Hellertown, PA 18055
(800) 334-WALE
Web site: www.waleapperatus.com

Northstar Glassworks, Inc.
9386 S.W. Tigard St.
Tigard, OR 97223
(866) 684-6986
Web site: www.northstarglass.com

L & K Tooling
350 Park Street
Waynesboro, PA 17268
(717) 762-1366

Glass Alchemy
Web site: www.glassalchemyarts.com

He says that for the next year or so he "lived the life of a starving artist who worked two jobs, designed logos, executed commissioned paintings, and created with anything and everything that I could get my hands on.

"Eventually, however, I realized that sitting behind a torch 40 hours a week, making hundreds of the same things, wasn't the life for me."

Chad quit his job and set up a lampworking studio in his house. There, equipped with a torch and ample newfound freedom, he began to experiment with colored borosilicate glass and vapors of metals.

"At first, I mostly made goblets, oil lamps, wedding cake tops and other custom pieces. Then one day I was asked to make a ring and bead for my girlfriend."

Since Chad had never seen anyone make a bead, and knew nothing of the craft, he once again was forced to experiment. After a few weeks of making several piles of "scrap glass," some gallery owners saw some prototypes of his beads in his studio and "they just couldn't seem to put them down." Chad was obviously creating something original.

Chad's beads are made by a unique process called "inside-out." Mandrels (the rods that hold beads during the melting process) are not used. Instead, intricate designs of colored borosilicate glass and vapors from precious metals are blown within a thick layer of clear glass and the whole thing reduced and annealed. The result is a beautiful one-of-a-kind bead that has a distinctive shape and colors deep and intense.

Chad's work is regularly shown at the Cristallo Art and Glass Gallery in Williamsburg, Virginia, and the Arts Afire Gallery in Alexandria. It has also been exhibited at The Bead Museum in Glendale, Arizona, and the prestigious Corning Museum of Glass in Corning, New York.

Now, with a successful career making and showing unique beads underway, Chad wants to add outreach to his program. He wants not only to create and promote glass art, but also to support environmental projects and art awareness programs in general. His goal is to inspire and evoke creativity in people from all walks of life. He has recently demonstrated glass working at inner city schools and several museums, for example. Chad is clearly a talented and multifaceted innovator in the field of lampwork beads. 🌀

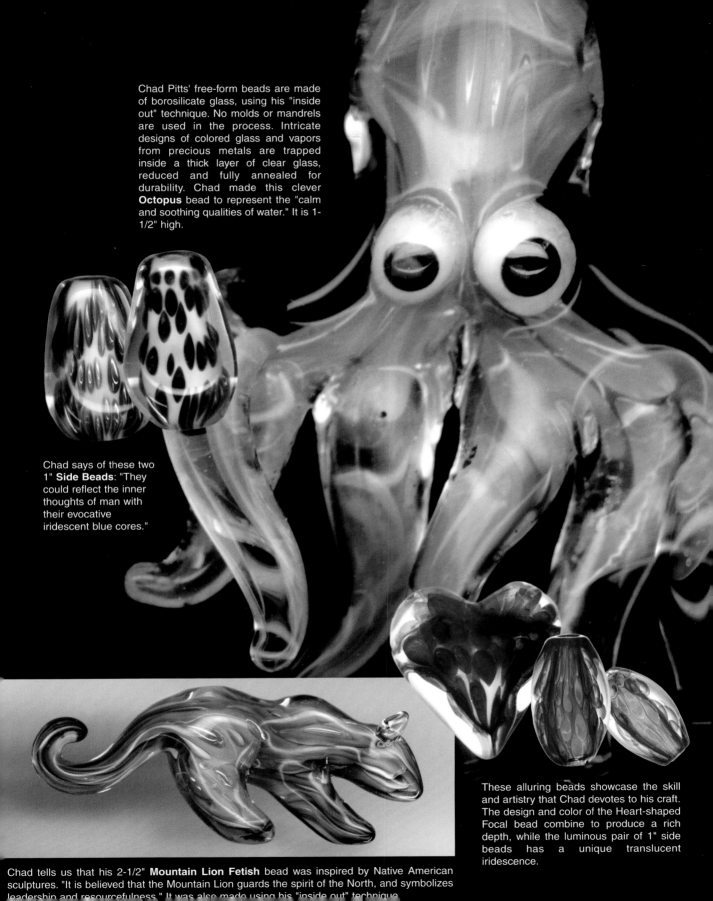

Chad Pitts' free-form beads are made of borosilicate glass, using his "inside out" technique. No molds or mandrels are used in the process. Intricate designs of colored glass and vapors from precious metals are trapped inside a thick layer of clear glass, reduced and fully annealed for durability. Chad made this clever **Octopus** bead to represent the "calm and soothing qualities of water." It is 1-1/2" high.

Chad says of these two 1" **Side Beads**: "They could reflect the inner thoughts of man with their evocative iridescent blue cores."

These alluring beads showcase the skill and artistry that Chad devotes to his craft. The design and color of the Heart-shaped Focal bead combine to produce a rich depth, while the luminous pair of 1" side beads has a unique translucent iridescence.

Chad tells us that his 2-1/2" **Mountain Lion Fetish** bead was inspired by Native American sculptures. "It is believed that the Mountain Lion guards the spirit of the North, and symbolizes leadership and resourcefulness." It was also made using his "inside out" technique.

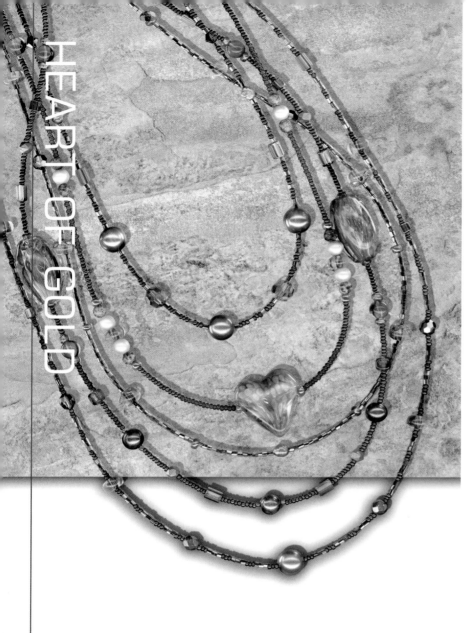

Necklace
Lampwork by Chad Pitts
Design by Susan Ray

The design, color, and shape of the heart-shaped focal bead combine to produce a rich depth, while the luminous pair of 1" side beads has a unique, translucent quality.

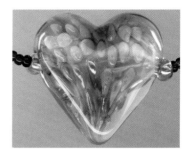

Supplies Needed

- Vermeil double hook "s" clasp
- 2 gold spring rings
- Vermeil wire, 6" length cut into two pieces
- 10 crimp beads
- 160" flexible wire

TIP: Make sure the spring rings fit comfortably into the vermeil cones.

TIP: Cut each length of wire 4" longer than the finished length to allow for crimping.

- Heart of Gold Heart bead, 25mm
- 2 side beads, 28mm
- 2 vermeil cones, 20mm
- 4 vermeil bell caps
- Assorted glass beads (rounds, discs and ovals), fresh water pearls, glass satin finished pearls, druks, faceted crystals, rectangle vitrails, and faceted bicones, 4mm to 10mm

TIP: String assorted beads 1" apart using seed or hex beads in between

- 2 strands of transparent rainbow chocolate cherry hex cuts
- 2 strands of bronze rocaille seed beads, 11/0
- Handful of transparent 6/0 bronze/topaz beads
- 10 vermeil balls (ending each length just before the crimp bead)

TIP: The color choices of light bronze, topaz, amethyst, light amethyst, light rose, iridescent purple, stone-finish browns, and color-lined deep rose and antique gold are all held together with bronze rocaille seed beads and transparent rainbow chocolate cherry hex cuts.

TIP: Each strand of the necklace is strung to the spring ring end. The spring ring is then placed inside of the vermeil cone and wired to the double hook "s" clasp with a length of vermeil wire.

Understated strands of tiny iridescent seed beads and 2mm to 8mm glass beads in warm earth tones and high finishes are used sparingly, allowing the eye to come to rest with the breathtaking beauty of Chad's Heart of Gold heart and side bead set.

How-to:
See Multi-strand
Necklaces in Basic How-
to Techniques, page 137.

INNER FIRE

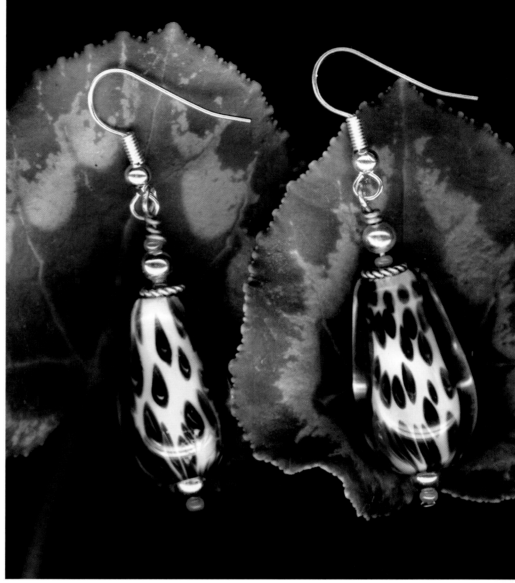

*These two 1"
side beads
reflect the inner
thoughts of man
with evocative
iridescent blue
cores.*

Finished length: 2-1/2"

Earrings
Lampwork by Chad Pitts
Design by Susan Ray

The iridescent blue cores shimmer with light as Chad's inside-out beads dance in the moonlight. Simple, elegant earring drops seemed like a natural choice to feature such a beautifully matched set of beads.

Supplies Needed

- 2 sterling silver ear wires with ball and coil
- 2 head pins 3" in length
- 4 sterling silver balls, 3mm
- 2 iridescent seed beads, 13/0
- 2 bali silver spacers

TIP: String the beads on each head pin and create the rosary turn right onto each ear wire. This was by far the fastest project to make but it looks like it took a lot of time and thought! Great stocking stuffer!

INNER FIRE

Glass can be given virtually any color by the addition of oxides of iron, cobalt, gold, copper, and other heavy metals. Cobalt, for example, makes for a blue glass, copper green, and gold a rose- to red-colored glass.

How-to:
See Rosary Turns in Basic How-to Techniques, page 138.

FAITH CHAPLET

Necklace
Lampwork by Trent and Shawn Warden
Design by Susan Ray

Never in my wildest dreams did I think that I would be making beads for a living ... I speak for both of us when I say that we feel truly blessed to be able to do lampwork for a living—something we both truly enjoy.

—Trent Warden

Both grew up in southern New Mexico, both have degrees in marketing from New Mexico State University, and, for the past couple of years, both have embraced lampworking as their love and livelihood. They are brothers Trent (orange shirt) and Shawn (blue shirt) Warden, who, when they are not tinkering with cars, manufacturing decorative water fountains or building kinetic gum ball machines (we kid you not!), are busy advancing their latest business, xbead.

Trent was the first to investigate lampworking as a possible profession after he happened across a Web page devoted to the subject while surfing the Internet one day. But before they could hang out a shingle, the brothers first had to convince themselves that they had a talent for glass bead making.

Their step into lampwork was considerably cushioned by several years' experience in making ceramic southwestern wall decor, a course given by noted lampworker Richard Inman (taken by Trent), reading all they could on the subject of beads, and a lot of time at the lamp.

"The hardest part was learning how to make a bead that was round," jokes Trent, recalling their beginnings in lampwork. "It seems like we spent most of our time just making or trying to make round beads. But in time we perfected the process."

Shawn says that his only training came from brother Trent. "From then on, it has been a hands on, trial and error experience," Shawn says. "Ceramic classes at New Mexico State University definitely helped me with the design aspects of bead making."

They both are pleased with the reception their beads are getting on Internet sites like eBay.

"Never in my wildest dreams did I think that I would be making beads for a living," exclaims Trent. "It's the most relaxing job I have ever had. I think it actually relieves my stress and calms me down. I speak for both of us when I say that we feel truly blessed to be able to do lampwork for a living—something we both truly enjoy."

Trent enjoys most the relaxing nature of bead making and says that when at the torch he is transported "to another world" where there is "only me and the glass."

"It's almost a hypnotic experience. All one's thoughts and worries are gone. I think what draws me most to lampworking is the manipulation of the glass. The things one can do with glass are endless. Watching the glass melt and cool to the shape of a bead is

ARTIST'S CONTACT INFORMATION

Trent and Shawn Warden
Xbead
POB 2335
Mesilla Park, NM 88047
(505) 527-5434
E-mail: xbead@zianet.com
eBay user ID: Xbead

Favorite Glass Supply Stores:
Frantz Art Glass & Supply
1222 E. Sunset Hill Road
Shelton, WA 98584
www.frantzartglass.com

Glass Alchemy, Ltd.
6539 NE 59th Place
Portland, OR 97218
www.glassalchemyarts.com

From previously working in ceramics, we both had experienced the firing process and what the process can create. It is quite a thrill to form and shape something in the mind and then throw in some luck and see what the outcome is.

—Trent Warden

fascinating. When the bead is in the flame and dots are being added to it, it looks like an alien spacecraft."

Shawn is also smitten by the mechanics of bead making. "Working with the glass, seeing it melt around the mandrel is quite exhilarating," he says. "It's quite amazing actually. What's really exciting about lampwork are the designs that just seem to happen.

"From previously working in ceramics, we both had experienced the firing process and what the process can create. It is quite a thrill to form and shape something in the mind and then throw in some luck and see what the outcome is. Like ceramics, lampwork is similar in the mystery of the outcome, but it is a lot quicker."

Both Trent and Shawn derive much of their inspiration from the colors and designs native to New Mexico.

"I try to open my eyes wherever I go for new ideas and colors," explains Trent. "The New Mexico sky, the diverse Indian and Mexican cultures are both continuous sources of ideas for both of us. Sky inspired bead sets are usually less symmetrical and more abstract. A lot of clear casing is used in these sets. Fuming with silver is used a lot too. Very rarely do I use silver or fumed silver in my symmetrical sets, only in the more abstract ones. Every day we try to do something different. New color combo's and designs—the possibilities are limitless!"

At the end of the day, though, the biggest kick the Wardens derive from their new-found art is the "work" itself.

"Going to work is like play time for me," says Trent. "I get to constantly experiment with new color combinations and designs all of the time. I really enjoy the many different shapes and endless colors. I enjoying building things, and bead making involves a process that uses lots of different tools and equipment. There are beads with twisties, dots, stacked dots, feathering, hollow beads, and so many more. How many people do you know that love what they do for a living?

"My brother is a lampworker as well as my business partner," enjoins Trent. "We challenge and inspire each other to come up with new and unique designs and techniques. Mom and Dad have started making beads as well. I guess it's a family affair. Mom and Dad have always supported our ideas, no matter how strange they where. We could not have done it without them."

Adds brother Shawn, "Lampwork gives me a way to express my artistic abilities through glass. It's very enriching to cherish what you do for a living as much as I do. It's great that we work together because we are each other's greatest asset." ❧

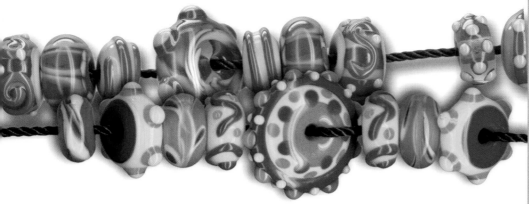

Carnival. The inspiration for this vibrant set of beads comes from the colors of the circus, says its maker Trent Warden. Made of Moretti glass, the colors are medium red, butter pastel yellow, and light lapis. Behind it, is **Palm Trees Sway**. The perfectly-matched colors of lapis, Nile green, and transparent blue echo the colors of a far-away tropical isle, says Trent.

Earth and Sky (immediate right) is made of turquoise, black, coral, and ivory Moretti glass encased in clear glass. The set is made using a fumed silver technique, which brings out the color. It was inspired, says Trent, by the beautiful New Mexico sky. **The Power of Purple** (far right) is Trent's purple and black set of Moretti glass beads reminiscent of the psychedelic '60s. "I think the bright purple says it all."

Closer Look (far left) and the **Beauty Within** (immediate left) are Shawn's contributions to the combined Warden output. Shawn says he never had any formal training in lampwork except for an hour's tutorial given to him by brother Trent.

"This set was inspired by the beautiful New Mexico sky," says maker Trent Warden.

Finished length: 14" from end to end (the chaplet doubles over in a continuous 16" loop)

Necklace
Lampwork by Trent and
Shawn Warden
Design by Susan Ray

Prayer beads have been among the many uses of beads throughout the centuries. These inspiring lampwork beads of turquoise, coral, black, and ivory Moretti glass encased in clear glass seemed to come from a different time and place. They are beautifully preserved and masterfully forged. A simple cross was used to highlight the lampwork. Vintage faceted onyx barrels and hand-cut crystal bicones complete the chaplet and pay homage to prayer.

Supplies Needed

- Sterling silver cross
- Sterling silver rosary connector
- Bali silver bauble, 10mm to 12mm
- 4 crimp beads
- 28" flexible wire
- 10 Moretti glass beads 10mm to 12mm
- 28 vintage faceted onyx barrels 6mm x 4mm
- Assorted crystal bicones
- Strand of 11/0 black seed beads
- 21 assorted complimentary seed beads (turquoise in 11/0 shown)
- 5 sterling silver balls (ending each length just before the crimp bead)

Tip: If you need more inspiration for chaplets and rosaries, please visit the rosary workshop at www.rosaryworkshop.com. Inspiration abounds!

How-to:
See Single-strand
Necklace in Basic How-to
Techniques, page 137.

BROTHERLY TIES

Inspiration for this bead set comes from the colors of a far away tropical isle.

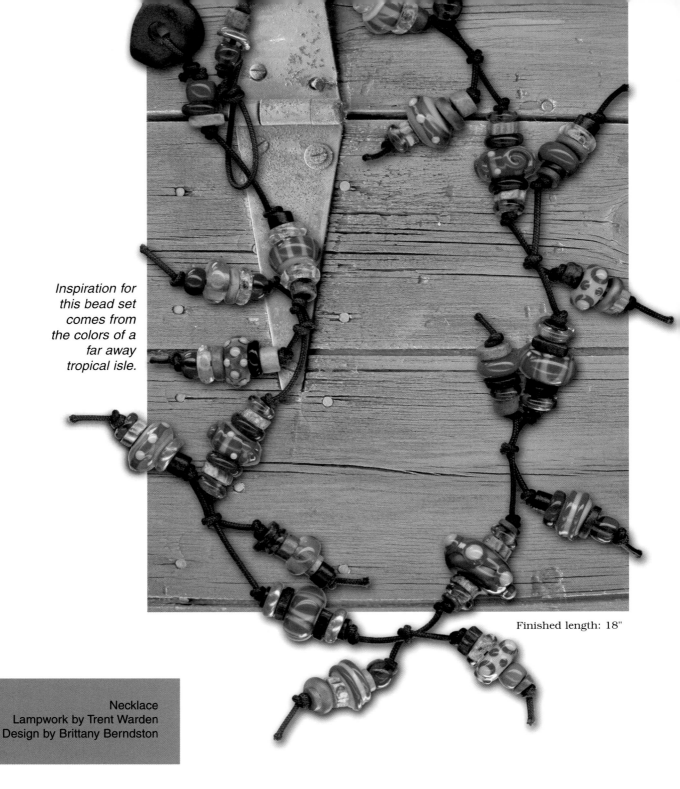

Finished length: 18"

Necklace
Lampwork by Trent Warden
Design by Brittany Berndston

Brittany is a young woman on her way to the College of the Atlantic. Brittany chose a contemporary design with strong lines and delicate leather tie features. It's a real winner, and so is she!

Supplies Needed

- 24" of leather cord
- 6 lengths of leather cord 6" long each
- 19 lampwork beads 8mm-20mm
- Assorted transparent and opaque glass beads 5mm-7mm
- 4 silver discs 6mm-8mm
- Ceramic bead for closure

How-to:
See Single-strand
Necklaces in Basic How-
to Techniques, page 137.

How-to:

Brittany's talents have given us a very simple leather cord necklace that we just could not resist using in the book. Create 21 bead groups from 5 to 7 beads each on your bead board. Set aside. Bring a loop through the ceramic disc that will be used for the closure. Make a square knot to secure. String the first group of beads securing in place with a second knot. Leave 1" of space between groupings. String on remaining groupings knotting before and after each bead group. Make a loop closure from the remaining leather cording.

To create the beaded drops, take one of the 6" lengths of cord and create a knot on one end. Bead on one of the bead groups and knot the other side. Now do the same for the other side of the cord. When complete you can tie it to the center of each 1" of leather cording. The lampwork and gravity will keep the drops in place. Repeat five more times.

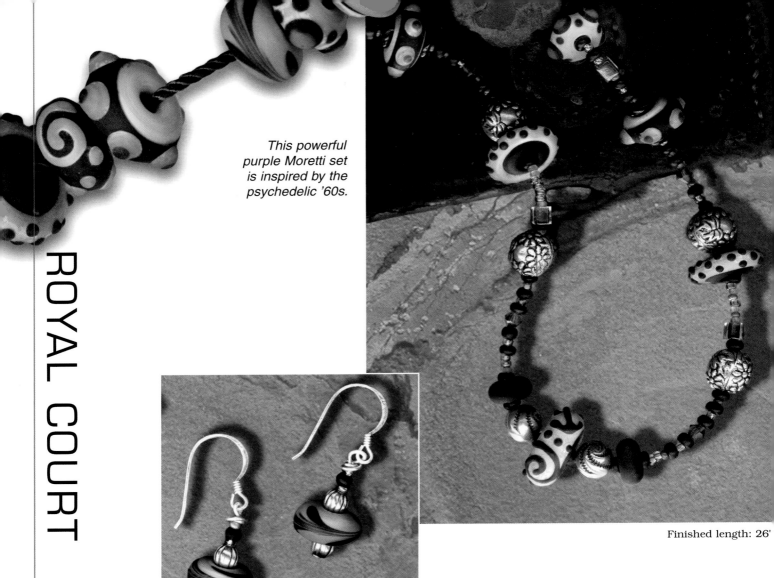

This powerful purple Moretti set is inspired by the psychedelic '60s.

ROYAL COURT

Finished length: 26'

Necklace and Earrings
Lampwork by Trent and Shawn Warden
Design by Pat Pauletto

Supplies Needed

- Sterling silver toggle clasp
- 2 crimp beads
- 30" flexible wire
- 17 Moretti glass beads, 10mm-18mm
- Strand of black matte seed beads, 8/0
- 4 silver colored triangle beads
- 6 aurora borealis finish bicones, 3mm x 6mm
- 8 color lined rectangles, 5mm x 3mm
- Strand seed bead mix, 11/0
- 18 bali silver round beads 4mm to 10mm
- 2 sterling silver balls (end each length just before the crimp bead)

Ear wires to match:
- 2 lampwork beads, 11mm
- 4 Bali silver beads, 4mm
- 2 black matte seed beads, 8/0
- 2 head pins, 3"
- 2 seed beads, 11/0

This is just a wonderful necklace. Pat showed her true romantic side, finishing the piece with the addition of delicate seed beads and color-lined rectangles.

How-to: See Single-strand
Necklaces in Basic How-to
Techniques, page 137; See
Rosary Turns in Basic How-
to Techniques, page 138.

ELEMENTS OF STRINGING

BASIC SINGLE-STRAND BRACELET

TIME NEEDED

The average time to complete any simple stringing project is approximately 30 minutes to 1 hour.

BASIC MATERIALS

- ***7-strand .018, silver-gray Beadalon∞ flexible wire***
One foot for a standard one-strand bracelet, and one yard for the longest of necklaces or lariats or eyeglass holders. We also recommend a yard if you are going to make a choker and a bracelet set.
- ***Sterling, gold, or vermeil crimp beads*** 2mm x 2 mm or 2mm x 3 mm
- ***Spring rings, silver or gold base metal***
- ***Silver, gold or vermeil 3mm-4mm seamless, round beads***
These beads are used to help finish your bracelets and necklaces. They are placed at each end of your project just before the crimp bead, which also means you will see them each time you put on or take off your jewelry. If they are seamless from the start, you won't ever be disappointed.
- ***Toggle or lobster clasp*** Toggle set or lobster claw clasp with tab end in gold, silver, base metal, pewter or vermeil (if tab end is not available you may use a jump ring or a string ring instead). Be careful when using pewter toggles. The metal is so soft and can easily be broken.
- ***2-4 headpins or eyepins*** 1" to 2" in length for attaching dangles, tassels or making earrings
- ***Containers*** Divided storage container or muffin tin or small jars for sorting beads.
- ***Bead boards*** Boards with at least three channels.
- ***Ear wires*** (if you would like to add coordinated earrings)
- ***Assorted Beads*** 20-60 beads depending on their size and length.

STANDARD TOOLS

- ***Flat edge Flat Nose Pliers*** Be sure they do NOT have a serrated surface as it will split right through the crimp beads.
- **Rosary or Needle Nose Pliers** The smaller the point the better the turn.
- ***Flat-sided wire cutters*** Have wire cutters dedicated only to your beading work, or you could become very frustrated. Make sure they are sharp and keep them in a clean, dry place.
- ***Notebook and colored pencils*** to retain ideas. Sometimes in setting out your beads you will stumble on to more than one pattern. It is a good idea to write down or draw your ideas for use on another project at a later time!

BRACELET DESIGN

Before I begin most projects, I try several arrangements of my beads on my bead board. Once you have chosen a fabulous art bead or set, make room for adventure! Using a white container, I will place my new acquisition in the center of the container and choose beads of varied size, shape, texture, sheen, transparency and color to "fill-in" my creation. Varying size, etc. can add more complexity to the work without the need to learn any fancy stringing techniques. Also, varying the color and transparency from the chosen art bead can heighten or soften it's appearance. Art beads will take center stage if you use more monochromatic tones and smaller beads in a complimentary color.

Where do you start? Let the art bead be your guide. Whatever appealed to you when you first chose your art bead, will help you to make your creation selections easily. If you get stumped, think about what outfit you might wear with this piece of jewelry, that may help you to chose additional colors for the work.

Once you have a fine assortment of beads (20 for a bracelet and 40 for a necklace) begin to lay your beads into a channel on the bead board. If you require a few more or a few less beads you can easily return to your bead box for more. You will come to know what pleases you by simple experimentation. There are an infinite number of patterns that you can use to make a simple bracelet.

In Line

A simple line of beads in a specific pattern running from one end of the bracelet to the other. There are many combinations you can create repeating bead after bead.

Centering: Start with the center bead and working each side from the center outward. I usually complete one side first and then simply match to the other side of the center bead.

Random: Using the "Sue Wilke" technique. Pile a handful of beads onto your bead board and then into the channel in the order they appear.

Seed Bead Fillers: I am very fond of using seed bead combinations to fill in between my focal beads. They add color without weight.

Making a simple one-strand bracelet with a flexible wire and toggle clasp closure is a good way to begin beadwork. If you have worked with hemp, elastic or memory wire before, you will enjoy the more finished look that metal closures and flexible wire can bring.

STEP BY STEP INSTRUCTIONS FOR SINGLE-STRAND BRACELETS

Use only real precious metal crimps; they hold up better. Sterling crimps are more flexible and respond easily to flattening. Base metal crimps can crack and wear, leaving you picking up handfuls of beads. Use the best flexible wire you can find. I prefer Beadalon. It is very strong, and very pliable. Beadalon comes in a number of colors, diameters and strengths. We used 7 strand .018, silver-gray Beadalon exclusively for all of the projects in this book. A list of suppliers is at the rear of the book, in case you have a problem finding any of the products recommended.

1. Cut 12" of flexible wire from spool.

2. To determine the size of your finished piece: Measure your wrist with a tape measure. Add 1" to your wrist measurement for the correct size of your finished bracelet. **Note:** If your beads are exceptionally large, you may need to add more than an inch to compensate for the additional diameter of the large beads.

3. In these instances, we will use a medical clamp to secure one end of the wire while we string. Then we can try the strung bracelet on before adding crimps and toggles. If the bracelet is too long, we can remove the medical clamp and remove a few beads. If it is too short, we can add a few beads.

4. To add the toggle closure to one end of the wire: String on crimp bead to one end of wire allowing it to slide 2" from the end of the flexible wire.

5. Now string one end of the clasp closure onto the wire. Most closures have a special ring for this attachment. you wish, you can add a jump ring or spring ring to the toggle or lobster claw. Be careful to make sure the diameter of the additional jump ring is small enough to easily fit through the toggle ring otherwise you will be unable to close it once upon your wrist.

6. If you are using a toggle, it is best to string the large end first. It will help when measuring for your final fit.

7. If you are using a lobster claw and tab, string the lobster claw first.

8. Holding the crimp bead in place, loop the wire back through the crimp bead.

9. Allow 2" of wire to pass through the crimp bead.

10. Pull the crimp bead up tight against the closure ring.

11. Using a flat nose pliers (not serrated), cover the crimp bead entirely.

12. Press down firmly on the crimp bead.

13. Spin the crimp bead around and press down firmly again. Your crimp bead should be uniformly flattened. Test the closure to be sure the crimp bead will hold by pulling firmly on the wire.

14. On your bead board, lay out approximately 7" of beads. (Most wrists are approximately 7". Your toggle clasp will account for 1" of your finished work. If your wrist size is more than 6," add additional beads to your length. If your wrist size is smaller, use fewer beads.) Your design can vary. Some people prefer consecutive patterns, others like random patterns. Work from the pattern illustration of one of our projects or note the pattern ideas below.

15. The first few beads on either end of your bracelet must accommodate both strands of wire, so you should avoid ending with seed beads. Try using a 6/0 or 8/0 bead for ending, if possible.

16. Once you are satisfied with your pattern, begin beading. Start by adding one 3mm-4mm silver or gold bead. String the metal bead through both strands of wire and place it up close to the crimp bead.

17. String on the first few beads. Pull back the long wire away from the bead and cut away the shorter wire. Discard this wire.

18. Now string on the remainder of your beads.

19. Examine your work; check that your short wire has remained strung within the first few beads, and that no beads are "hung up" on the wire. If this is your first bracelet, it is now time to try it on! Holding the open end firmly (or ask someone else to hold it for you), wrap the bracelet around your wrist to see if your measurements were accurate. Sometimes beads resting on the bead board actually require less room once strung. This especially happens with gemstone chips. At rest, the chips will appear to occupy more space than they actually do.

20. Once you have completed a bracelet that fits you properly and know exactly where you would like it to rest on your arm, you can use this bracelet for a pattern for other bracelets you would like to make. This is still a "trial and error" technique. Everyone has an imaginary point on his or her wrists that feels right. Younger wearers might prefer a bracelet that is worn with a more snug fit. Some men like their bracelets worn higher on their arms, away from their watchbands. Most women seem to prefer the bracelet to rest at the wrist joint, just showing below a cuff line. Everyone does have their own preferences, so best to have the wearer try on a few bracelets before making one for a friend. Remember too, that larger beads usually take up more depth as well as length and you may need to experiment to get the fit right when making a bracelet with larger beads on it.

21. When all the beads are in place, add the remaining silver or gold metal bead and the remaining crimp bead.

22. Holding the crimp bead in place, string on the opposite end of your clasp.

23. Now, loop the wire back through the crimp bead, this time stringing it through two additional beads as you go.

24. Once the wire clears the second bead, you can begin to pull the wire taut. **Note:** It is easiest to pull the wire through the crimp, silver bead and end beads, if you can keep the crimp bead AWAY from the clasp end as you go. Sometimes, if enough wire remains, you can simple feed the loop until most the wire has been strung in place. Other times you will need the aid of the needle nose pliers to hold the end of the wire and pull it through the beads as you go.

25. Once the wire has been pulled as far as possible, you should check your beads from the other end of the bracelet. Holding the finished end down, make sure no space remains between any of the beads. Sometimes a bead will get "hung up" on the wire and more often than not, won't be discovered until after you have crimped your second crimp bead unless you take the time here to inspect your work.

26. Once all is well, pull once again on your wire for a final fit. Cover the crimp bead with the needle nose pliers and then press down firmly. Flip your crimp bead over and apply the same pressure to the opposite side. Now tug slightly on the beads to be sure the crimp is in place properly.

27. Separate the beads where the small wire rests into a 45-degree angle. Cut away the shorter strand of wire by holding the flat side of your wire cutters to the bead. Even the smallest little wire bit remaining can cause irritation to the wrist! So, it's best to cut really close. Make sure the beaded wire remains away from the cutters, or you will have to do this all again!

28. Now try it on again. Hopefully it is a fit. If not, just cut away the wire below the silver bead and restring it again. All you have lost is two crimp beads and a little time. Add or subtract the beads to make it a perfect fit!

29. Once your bracelet is complete, I would suggest that you put it on a flat bed scanner and scan the bracelet full size. It is fun to note the exact size of the bracelet, the date it was made, the person who owns it, what types and origins of the beads and where the beads where purchased. You can even keep a scrapbook of all of the beaded work you do! It will be a fond memory of how much you will learn over the years ahead as well as a document as to where many beads originated.

To complete a multi strand bracelet you will repeat the instructions, below, for each strand of the bracelet, completing one strand at a time.

1. Cut 12" of wire from the spool.

2. Measure your wrist, adding 1" for the finished length.

3. String one crimp bead, looping it through the larger end of the clasp and back through the crimp bead. Pull the crimp bead taut. Crimp it. Check to be sure it is secure.

Note: When making multi-strands, you must keep the wire loop with each consecutive strand in the same order on each side of the bracelet.

4. Lay out your pattern of beads.

5. String both wires through the precious metal bead and two or three glass beads, then cut the excess "tail" of wire away with your wire cutters.

6. String the remainder of the beads.

7. Check the length of the bracelet for proper fit.

8. String the precious metal bead and the other crimp bead. Loop the flexible wire through the ring on the other end of the toggle and back through the crimp bead, the precious metal bead and two or three glass beads.

9. Work with the flexible wire until you have made it taunt. Check that all the beads are in place. (Sometimes a bead can slip and leave a gap of wire. Hold the strand vertically and pull on each bead to be sure it is not hung up somewhere.)

10. Crimp the second crimp bead in place. Check to be sure it is secure.

11. Cut away the excess "tail" of wire.

12. Continue to follow these instructions for each consecutive strand.

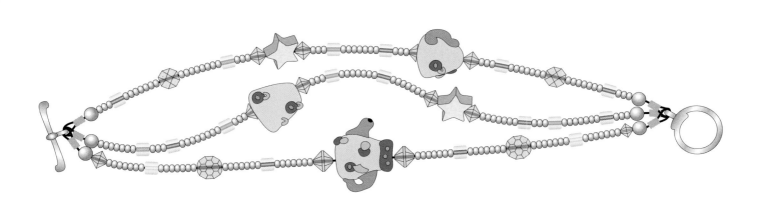

To complete a necklace or choker, the instructions remain the same as with a bracelet. If you choose to make a multi-strand necklace, you will repeat the above instructions for each strand of the necklace, completing one strand at a time.

1. Determine the length of the necklace desired. Add 4 inches to the necklace to complete the closure. You will cut away the excess when the piece is completed.

2. Cut wire from the spool.

3. String one crimp bead, looping it through the larger end of the clasp and back through the crimp bead. Pull the crimp bead taunt. Crimp it. Check to be sure it is secure. **Note:** When making multi-strands, you must keep the wire loop with each consecutive strand in the same order on each side of the necklace.

4. Lay out your pattern of beads. **Note:** Remember to vary your colors, textures, transparency, size and shape of your beads when building your necklace.

5. String both wires through the precious metal bead and two or three glass beads, then cut the excess "tail" of wire away with your wire cutters.

6. String the remainder of the beads.

7. Check the length of your necklace for proper fit.

8. String the precious metal bead and the other crimp bead to the end of the necklace. Loop the flexible wire through the ring on the opposite end of the toggle and back through the crimp bead, the precious metal bead and two or three glass beads.

9. Work with the flexible wire until you have made it taunt. Check that all the beads are in place. (Sometimes a bead can slip and leave a gap of wire. Hold the strand vertically and pull on each bead to be sure it is not hung up somewhere.)

10. Crimp the second crimp bead in place. Check to be sure it is secure.

11. Cut away the excess "tail" of wire.

12. Continue to follow these instructions for each consecutive strand.

BASIC MATERIALS
- Sterling or vermeil head pins in 2" lengths
- PRACTICE does make perfect. The best suggestion is that you take the time to practice this technique. Most people must turn at least 50 dangles before they can say that they have accomplished the rosary turn. Using finer wire is essential to getting the proper look of the turn. I recommend the wire hardness of ? hard and the gauge of .22.

STANDARD TOOLS
- Rosary or needle nose pliers (Tip: The smaller, more delicate the cone on the needle nose pliers, the better the results).
- Sharp wire cutters.
- Flat nose pliers.

Supplies Needed

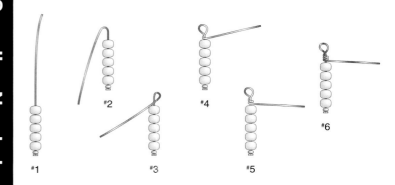

STEP-BY-STEP INSTRUCTIONS FOR MAKING ROSARY TURNS

1. Let's begin with a dangle, which is prepared first and added to your necklace as you string it. It is a lot easier to work "off-line" when learning this technique. Once you have the technique down, you can actually do them on the earring wires or necklace at the same time.

2. Gather beads to "string" on the head pin.

3. String the beads onto the head pin using the tiny head of the beads as the base of the dangle. (If your first bead is too large and falls off the tiny head, try stringing a small transparent 10/0, 8/0 or 6/0 seed bead on the end first. This will help hold the larger bead in place. Leave approximately 1" of the pin showing.

4. Once all of your beads are strung, place your needle nose pliers approximately 1/4" from the top of the last bead. Grasp the pin tightly with the pliers.

5. Using your thumb and forefinger, bend the wire over and cross in front of the stationary wire forming the start of the loop.

6. Next, bring the wire forward beginning the first complete turn.

7. We have had the best success by grasping the newly formed loop with the pliers and turning the loop several times to provide three neatly placed turns. Some people choose to turn the wire instead of the loop, but in our experience, we have had the best results by turning the loop itself. This seems to give a much tighter finish to the work.

8. When the turns are completed, cut away the remainder of the wire.

9. Grasping the loop with the rosary pliers, tuck the newly cut end down and in toward the top bead with your flat nose.

10. Now your dangle is complete and the loop can be strung onto the wire as if it were any other bead.

11. As I mentioned, once you have accomplished the rosary turn, you should practice doing the turn onto the loop of a pair of fishhook earrings. This is easily accomplished with a little patience.

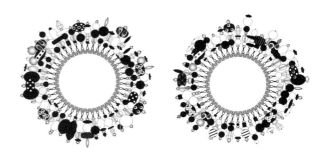

TO ADD TASSELS TO YOUR WORK

If you would like to add a tassel to the clasp of your necklace or bracelet or dangle a hundred beads on a cha-cha bracelet, this method will get your well on your way. It does take practice and some patience. Don't give up! Once you have accomplished the turn you will be able to make about 50 pairs of earrings while watching your favorite flick (which can come in handy if you have a lunch group you would like to do something special for, or an exceedingly long Christmas list).

The "Tool Box"

We recommend that you create a standard toolbox for all of your creative jewelry work. It should include the following items:

- Single or multi-strand flocked gray bead board
- 12 part storage box for sorting beads
- .018 flexible wire—which comes in spools of 30 ft., 100 ft. or 1000 ft.
- Jeweler's tools: Needle nose pliers, rosary or internal pliers and good, sharp wire cutters
- Big eye needles—TIP: Have several BIG EYE needles on hand, they are such wonderful needles you will wear them out!
- Nymo thread—white and black, available in approximately 3000 yard spools or smaller bobbins. Sizes A through D.
- Jewelry glue—useful for loose rhinestones.
- Quick glue—just a touch of quick glue can save your life sometimes!
- Adequate lighting. We use an OTT-LITE True Color Lamp which helps to see details and match colors clearly. It also reduces eye strain. Check your local bead or craft store for various styles. Magnifier lamps are also available.

Supplies Needed

Tools

Your jewelry toolbox should include Flat Nose Pliers, Rosary (or Internal Pliers) and a good pair of wire cutters. Titanium wire cutters, although expensive, are a worthwhile investment. If you are on a budget, there is no need to invest in tools specifically made for jewelry. Your hardware store carries tools that are adequate for the work. Buy tools that are comfortable in your hand. I prefer the shorter, foam-covered handles. Look for delicate cones on your Rosary pliers. The refinement will help you make even the smallest loops.

Bead Boards, Storage Boxes, Needles, NYMO & Tools

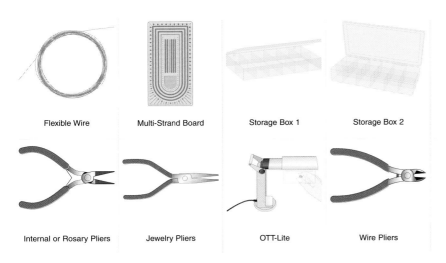

Flexible Wire   Multi-Strand Board   Storage Box 1   Storage Box 2   Three Strand Board   Big Eye Needles   NYMO

Internal or Rosary Pliers   Jewelry Pliers   OTT-Lite   Wire Pliers

Findings

Jewelry findings are available at craft and bead stores. With some luck, you can find wonderful vintage findings at thrift and resale shops. A cardinal rule: Don't skimp on crimps! Crimps are available in many weights and materials. Use crimp beads in sterling in at least half-hard silver and heavier gauge wire. Available from bead stores and bead distributors, these crimps are more expensive but worth every penny. Quality crimps will ensure you will enjoy your new beaded jewelry for years to come. I prefer 2mm x 3mm and 2mm x 2mm, half hard, sterling silver crimps in heavier gauge wire for the majority of my work. I recommend that you add a sterling or gold plate 2mm to 3mm ball to the end of your stringing right before your crimp bead. The additional ball helps support the wear and tear each crimp bead takes. String the flexible wires back through the crimp bead, ball, and at least 1" of beads before cutting away the short end.

Ear wires are available in many styles. Try on ear wires before buying too many. Many styles of ear wires fit the ear differently. Surgical steel and sterling are best for sensitive ears. Clasps are also available in many new styles. If you prefer toggles, be sure that the bar end is larger than the loop end. This will help ensure that the toggle stays in place when you wear your jewelry. Make sure the first few beads nearest the bar end will slip comfortably through the loop end or you won't be able to use the toggle closure without a struggle.

Chains

| 2.2 mm ball chain | 2.2 mm cable chain | 2.5 mm fine curb chain | 3.2 mm medium curb chain | 3.4mm curb chain | 5.5 mm twisted cable chain |

Jewelry Fittings

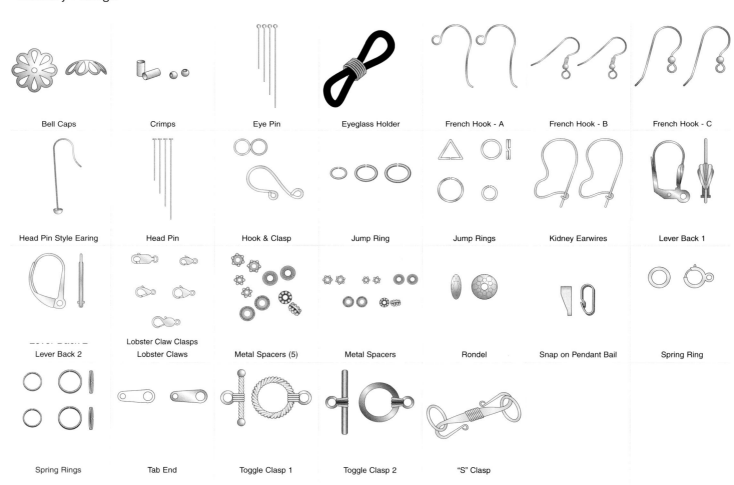

Bell Caps | Crimps | Eye Pin | Eyeglass Holder | French Hook - A | French Hook - B | French Hook - C

Head Pin Style Earing | Head Pin | Hook & Clasp | Jump Ring | Jump Rings | Kidney Earwires | Lever Back 1

Lever Back 2 | Lobster Claw Clasps / Lobster Claws | Metal Spacers (5) | Metal Spacers | Rondel | Snap on Pendant Bail | Spring Ring

Spring Rings | Tab End | Toggle Clasp 1 | Toggle Clasp 2 | "S" Clasp

How many beads do you need? A simple way to figure out how many beads your necklace will require is to take a sampling of the beads you are planning to use and line them up on your bead board. Divide 4 into your desired finished length. Cover a four-inch length. Count the number of beads that will be required to cover a 4" length. Then multiply your number of beads by the finished length of the necklace or bracelet.

Example: If it takes 12 beads to fill the four inch length and you want your finished necklace to be 16", divide 4" by 16 = 4 and then multiply 12 x 4 = 48 beads to complete your piece.

USE YOUR BEAD BOARD! The board offers accurate measurements for multiple necklaces as well allowing you to change beads order or even change the type of beads used without disturbing your design work.

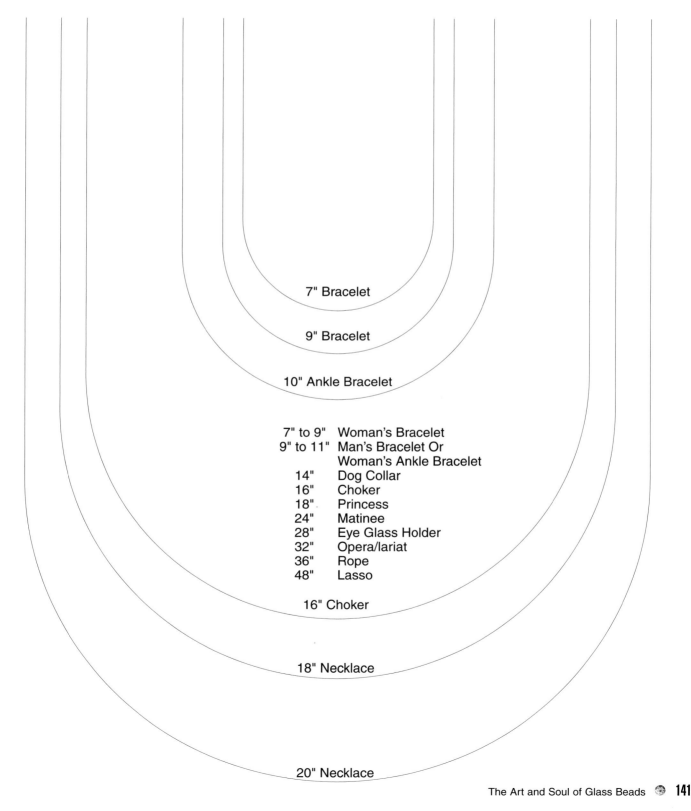

7" Bracelet

9" Bracelet

10" Ankle Bracelet

7" to 9"	Woman's Bracelet
9" to 11"	Man's Bracelet Or Woman's Ankle Bracelet
14"	Dog Collar
16"	Choker
18"	Princess
24"	Matinee
28"	Eye Glass Holder
32"	Opera/lariat
36"	Rope
48"	Lasso

16" Choker

18" Necklace

20" Necklace

Beads

Beads abound. Study the shape, facets, and finishes. Many beads are priced based on the composition of the bead, origin, and quality. Just as with diamonds, beads can be rated by their color, transparency, number of facets, and the like. Make a note of the country of origin. It is fun to use beads from faraway places. Craft stores have large varieties of beads if you do not have a local bead shop in your area. Lampwork is harder to find in many areas and can be more expensive than the copies craft stores offer. Handmade lampwork is unique and often only one of a kind is available. You will easily find lampwork online at auctions and at many artists' own Web sites. Use your favorite search engine to hunt for "lampwork" or "glass beads." Study bead magazines. Many artists and distributors advertise in *Bead and Button*, *Beadworks*, and other bead magazines.

Finishes

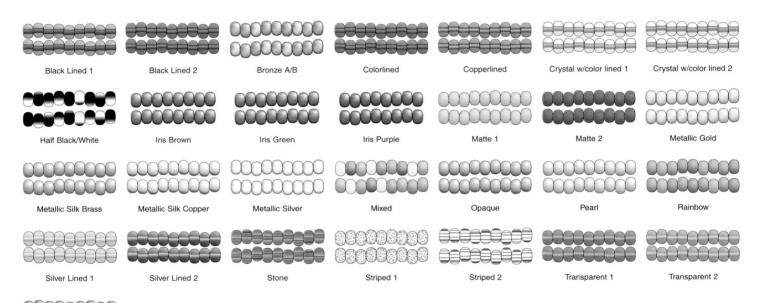

Black Lined 1 · Black Lined 2 · Bronze A/B · Colorlined · Copperlined · Crystal w/color lined 1 · Crystal w/color lined 2

Half Black/White · Iris Brown · Iris Green · Iris Purple · Matte 1 · Matte 2 · Metallic Gold

Metallic Silk Brass · Metallic Silk Copper · Metallic Silver · Mixed · Opaque · Pearl · Rainbow

Silver Lined 1 · Silver Lined 2 · Stone · Striped 1 · Striped 2 · Transparent 1 · Transparent 2

White Heart

Pressed Glass

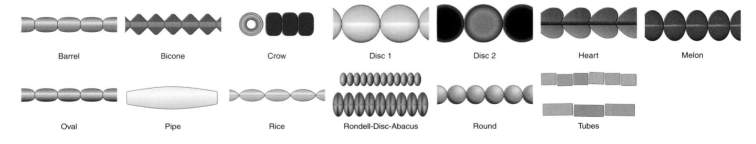

Barrel · Bicone · Crow · Disc 1 · Disc 2 · Heart · Melon

Oval · Pipe · Rice · Rondell-Disc-Abacus · Round · Tubes

Fire Polished

Bicone 3mm · Bicone 5mm · Cathedral · Faceted Disc · Faceted Drop · Faceted Round · Fancy Cathedral

Leaves/Fancy Shapes

Size & Shape Samples

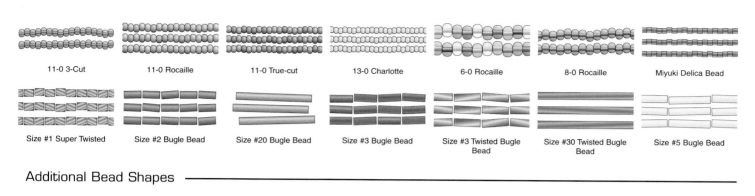

| 11-0 3-Cut | 11-0 Rocaille | 11-0 True-cut | 13-0 Charlotte | 6-0 Rocaille | 8-0 Rocaille | Miyuki Delica Bead |

| Size #1 Super Twisted | Size #2 Bugle Bead | Size #20 Bugle Bead | Size #3 Bugle Bead | Size #3 Twisted Bugle Bead | Size #30 Twisted Bugle Bead | Size #5 Bugle Bead |

Additional Bead Shapes

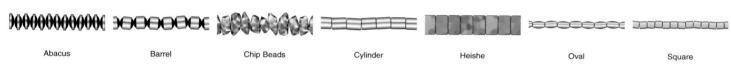

| Abacus | Barrel | Chip Beads | Cylinder | Heishe | Oval | Square |

Bead Sizes

Metric is the name of the game when it comes to beads. Beads come from all over the world, and since the metric system is used elsewhere, beads are measured in millimeters more often than not. If you never were a fan of metric, here are simple charts to help you make the transition. Be sure to keep your chart handy when buying beads online. Photos can offer distort the size of a bead. Be sure to read the fine print when purchasing beads online or in catalogs.

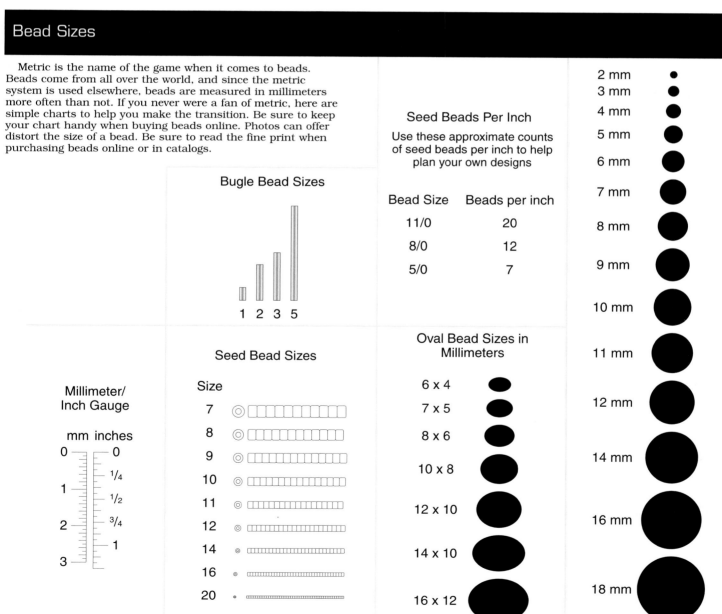

Seed Beads Per Inch

Use these approximate counts of seed beads per inch to help plan your own designs

Bead Size	Beads per inch
11/0	20
8/0	12
5/0	7

Bugle Bead Sizes

1 2 3 5

Seed Bead Sizes

Size
7
8
9
10
11
12
14
16
20

Millimeter/Inch Gauge

mm inches

Oval Bead Sizes in Millimeters

6 x 4
7 x 5
8 x 6
10 x 8
12 x 10
14 x 10
16 x 12

2 mm
3 mm
4 mm
5 mm
6 mm
7 mm
8 mm
9 mm
10 mm
11 mm
12 mm
14 mm
16 mm
18 mm

About the Authors

Susan Ray has been a creative, innovative and positive force for a number of retail companies throughout her career, serving as executive director and vice president of product development and merchandise manager for companies such as Ideaforest, the Internet development company for JoAnn's Fabrics, Import Connections, White Rose Nurseries, Ben Franklin Retail Stores, and part of the buying staff for Frederick Atkins, and Peck and Peck, New York.

Susan shows a keen eye for identifying emerging consumer market trends, in-depth understanding of consumer marketing and strategic planning. An entrepreneur, Susan has founded Artinteriors, Cirq Art de Vivre and notably, Cyberplay, a children's computer exploration center which was honored with a ComputerWorld Smithsonian Award for heroic innovation of technology.

Her homes have been featured in *Crafts* magazine, *Country Sampler*, *Craft & Home* magazine, *CS's Christmas Decorating Ideas*. Many of her designs have been published in *Better Homes and Gardens, Country Crafts, Country Handicrafts, Woman's Day, McCall's Needlework and Crafts, Crafts magazine, Harris Publications, Bridal Crafts* magazine, Oxmoor House, *PCM* magazine, Hot Off the Press Publications, The Finish Line, Plaid Publications, Suzanne McNeil, and Maxwell International.

Currently, Susan is enjoying her new home in Galena, Illinois, and using her time to form a franchise company for her bead store, Bubbles, Bangles, and Beads. She can be reached on the Web at raysa@www.bubblesbanglesbeads.com.

Richard Pearce is a writer, photographer, conservationist, and former medical researcher. For more than eight years, he investigated the genetic causes of diabetes and other autoimmune diseases. Richard has also worked as a free lance science writer and, in that capacity, authored hundreds of articles for national magazines on subjects ranging from renewable energy to the many uses of aspirin.

Recently, Richard moved to Illinois, where the views of the prairie—especially extraordinary close-up images—astonished and delighted him. He is currently compiling a catalog of upper Mississippi wild flowers. The methods developed for that project were used to photograph this book.